Emotional Literacy

Emotional Literacy

KEEPING YOUR HEART

Educating Your Emotions and
Learning to Let Them Educate You

FRANCIS F. SEEBURGER

A Crossroad Book
The Crossroad Publishing Company
New York

1997

The Crossroad Publishing Company
370 Lexington Avenue, New York, NY 10017

Printed in the United States of America

Library of Congress Cataloging-in-Publication Data
Seeburger, Francis F.
    Emotional literacy : keeping your heart : educating your emotions
and learning to let them educate you / by Francis F. Seeburger.
        p.   cm.
    ISBN 0-8245-1607-9 (pb)
    1. Emotions (Philosophy)   I. Title.
    B105.E46S44   1997
    128'.37–dc21   97-6809
                                                            CIP

To my son,

AARON,

in memory of his grandfather, my father,
CHARLES JAMES SEEBURGER

Contents

Preface

The idea for this book has been growing in my mind for the last five or six years. During that time many people helped me develop my thoughts in conversation. I never even knew the names of some of them — individuals who brought me a valuable insight by way of what may have seemed to them at the time to be no more than a passing comment, or simply by providing me a willing ear when I needed one. There are others whose names I have forgotten. Even those whose names I not only once knew, but have also managed to remember, are too numerous for me to thank each of them here by name.

I am grateful to them all, known and unknown, remembered and forgotten.

There are also a handful of individuals who directly made significant contributions to my work during the time I was actually writing. Each of them deserves to be thanked by name.

Bill Anderson, my colleague and friend of many years in the Philosophy Department at the University of Denver, read drafts of the manuscript and gave me valuable suggestions. So did Russ Shaw, a more recent but no less valued friend from outside the academic community.

Trish Dunn has given me much spiritual guidance over the course of the gestation and composition of this book. She was also kind enough to read drafts of the chapters as I wrote them. I could always count on her to give me useful criticism along with unflagging encouragement.

Pat Bethke has been a good and reliable support to me throughout the period that I was developing my thoughts, then writing this book. We have talked about the material covered in the book on many occasions over the last few years. More importantly, as my friend of a decade, Pat has herself accompanied me on some of the longest stretches of my personal journey into emotional literacy. Finally, she also read drafts of the chapters as I was composing them and gave me helpful, supportive criticism.

Mike Leach, my publisher, has had faith in me and this project from the beginning of the actual writing. He has always been ready with suggestions and support. Without his good judgment and excellent editorial advice, the finished book would have been very different.

Finally, my wife, Gayle, upheld me throughout the process of imagining, nurturing, developing, writing, and revising the book, as she has always done for all my writing during more than a quarter-century of marriage. She reads whatever I write, however long-winded or abstruse, and always makes careful criticism. Most of all she offers me the love and support without which I would not be able to continue writing in the first place.

I give thanks to, and for, them all.

Introduction

Keep thy heart with all diligence, for out of it are the issues of life.

– PROVERBS 4:23

This book is about keeping the heart. It contains basic lessons in emotional literacy.

Especially in matters of the heart, the best way to teach is by example. Accordingly, at the center of the book is my own story of how, for the last decade, I have been developing my own emotional literacy — learning how to keep my own heart.

During that time one of the things I have learned about my own heart is that I am an episodic storyteller. For the life of me, I can't seem to tell a story in standard chronological form, from beginning through middle to end. Instead, whenever I try to tell a story, I find myself jumping around from one part of the story to another, taking an episode here and an episode there. I seem unable to tell the story of a journey — and all stories are stories of journeys, finally — except by offering up what may often appear to be no more than random impressions and anecdotes gathered along the journey's way. In this book I am true to myself in the episodic way I tell the story of my own journey into emotional literacy.

In the pages that follow I am also true to myself and my own ways as a storyteller in at least one other important regard: the story I tell is above all an intellectual one, in the best and highest sense of that too often abused word. It is a story of ideas. All of my life I have lived the life of ideas, "the life of the mind." I have no desire to change that now, when I am in the midst of midlife, despite the crises to which midlife is popularly (and in my own case, at least, quite rightly) said to be prone.

Thus, the bulk of this book takes the form of sustained reflections on some of the emotions, reflections that helped lead me along the way on my own journey to emotional literacy. I can personally vouch for each of them. In agreement with the nineteenth-century German philosopher Friedrich Nietzsche's idea that the only thoughts worth thinking are those one is willing to try living by, I have not only thought them all in some abstract sense of thinking, but also lived them concretely. Nietzsche also says that one's thoughts should give off a strong scent, like a ripe cornfield. I hope that, at least at times, the following pages carry the hint of such fragrance, at least to some readers' noses.

In the most basic and ancient sense of the word, this is a book of "philosophy" — not philosophy as academic scholarship, but philosophy as the love of wisdom. As the love of wisdom philosophy is a way of life, and, as Socrates taught, the philosophical life is the only fully human way to live. It is the only way of life that can truly succeed in keeping the heart.

So that no one need be frightened away from reading it by my labeling the book a work of "philosophy," let me hasten to add that it is also — indeed, above all — a book concerned with personal growth. It is a book both *of* and *for* recovery and healing. It is "of" them in that it is the result of my own recovery and healing, an expression of my own growth over the last decade, especially. It is "for" recovery and healing in that my purpose in writing it is to offer others some important lessons for their own recovery and healing, their own personal growth — the growth of the "heart." An alternative translation of the verse from Proverbs which opens this Introduction advises the reader to "guard" the heart rather than to "keep" it. A third translation uses "protect." Yet another has "watch over." In the Christian Gospels Jesus repeatedly tells his disciples that moment by moment they must maintain a vigilant watchfulness, for they do not know when the kingdom of God may come upon them, and woe to anyone caught napping when it does.

Philosophy as a way of life is the practice of such watchfulness. the ancient Christian desert fathers and mothers were all called philosophers in the original sense. The tradition they established has survived to this day in Eastern Orthodox Christianity. As it is put in some of the texts collected together in the *Philokalia* (a compilation of writings over the centuries by contemplatives honored in the Orthodox church), to maintain the sort of watchfulness at issue in the life of such philosophers it is necessary to "put the mind in the heart," and then to keep it there.

Unfortunately, in the Latin Christian tradition and the secular Western culture that eventually developed out of it, that formula tended to be reversed. The heart was put in the mind. "Reason" was rigidly separated from emotion, passion, and all else that pertained to the heart. In turn, reason was assigned solely to the head. Then, finally, the head was declared absolute monarch, to which the heart was supposed to owe unquestioning fealty.

It would please me greatly if, by offering the following basic lessons in keeping the heart, I were to help even a handful of readers begin to put their heads back in their hearts, where they have always belonged. That is the crucial first step toward developing emotional literacy.

By "emotional literacy" I mean something twofold. First, becoming emotionally literate is *developing one's capacity to feel the full range of human emotions.* Second, it is *learning to feel the emotions appropriate to the actual situations in which we find ourselves moment by moment.*

To be literate is to be able to read. To be emotionally literate is to be able to "read" the emotions themselves. To do that, we must first be able to tell them apart (tell anger from fear or frustration, for example), just as we first have to learn to recognize the individual words when we learn to read in the ordinary sense. In terms of emotional literacy, that is a matter of developing our capacity to feel the full range of emotion, the first part of my definition of "emotional literacy."

Once we've learned how to tell individual words apart and to recognize each word in turn, we then have to learn how to follow the sequences of words as they combine together to form sentences. In just the same way, to become emotionally literate we have to go beyond merely feeling the various emotions themselves. We have to learn how they combine with one another in specific circumstances to form our actual affective (a word that means of or pertaining to emotions, feelings, moods, and the like) responses to the various life-situations in which we find ourselves as we go through our days.

We could say that becoming emotionally literate in the twofold sense I've just explained is coming to have a "well-read heart." We can give that expression — a well-read heart — a rich, double sense, in order to use it as such a symbol for emotional literacy.

On the one hand, we can use the expression "a well-read heart" the way we talk about a "well-read book," meaning a book that has been read over and over again many times. In that sense, a well-read heart would be one that had been "read" often and carefully by someone attentive to his or her own emotional responses to the world. It would be a heart that had been opened often, and that had taught its reader much.

On the other hand, we can talk about a heart itself being "well read" the way we might say that of some person. A well-read person is not a person who has *been* read well and often, but one who has herself or himself *done* a lot of reading, and done it "well," which means with good breadth and depth across a variety of kinds of literature and subject matters. In the same way, a well-read heart would be a heart that had itself been exposed to a wide variety of carefully selected emotional "material." It would be a heart that had felt "widely and well."

Putting the two together, a "well-read heart" would be a heart that had been carefully developed, and that in turn had been carefully heeded by the person whose heart it was, for the sake of that person's own development. It would be a heart both well tended, and well attended to. To have a well-read heart would be to have cultivated one's heart well, and to have been well cultivated by it in turn.

In addition to having lived my whole life as a life of ideas, I have also lived my whole adult life as that of a university classroom teacher. My years of teaching college classes to students from freshman to doctoral level (and from teenagers to septuagenarians) have taught me how important repetition and reinforcement are for learning, and how necessary it is often to call students' attention to things they should notice and remember in what they are studying. Students themselves may be all too quick to ask, "Will this be on the test?" — and to dismiss whatever won't be (although that includes all the truly important things, which can never be put in a classroom test). Despite how easily it can be abused, however, that question still reflects the important point that when we are learning we need help separating what deserves attending to and remembering from what doesn't.

For that reason, I've interspersed what I hope will be useful condensations, reviews, and other aids throughout the narrative. These insertions provide a running summary of the main points that emerge in the text.

AIDS FOR THE READER

I've put all that sort of material within rules, as you see here, just as I might on a chalkboard in one of my classes.

Also based on my classroom experience, after my own personal narrative in each chapter I've put a section called "Self-Evaluation," containing questions you can ask yourself in order to assess your own level of emotional literacy. By reflecting carefully on these questions as directed, you can begin to learn what you personally need to work on if you want to become more adept at keeping your own heart.

Finally, at the very end of each chapter I've included a section containing suggested disciplines, practices, and exercises for you to incorporate into your own daily life. They are all proven, tradition-grounded, concrete ways in which you can cultivate your own emotional literacy, if you are willing to commit to them. What you learn from reflecting on the questions from the preceding "Self-Evaluation" sections will help you decide which of these suggested disciplines, practices, and exercises are most suited to your own individual needs.

– One –

Emotional Literacy: Learning How to Feel

When I was forty years old, I had to start learning how to feel. I am not alone. There are many of us today — people who, well into adulthood, have still not learned how to feel. Some of us never do. In contemporary consumer societies, especially here in America, we form a great mass of the emotionally illiterate.

At length I pass to the remaining portion of my Ethics, which is concerned with the way leading to freedom. I shall therefore treat therein of the power of the reason, showing how far the reason can control the emotions.　　　　　　　　　　　　　　　　– Spinoza, *Ethics*

There are many reasons for my own emotional illiteracy, most of them common enough. For one thing, I am an heir of the dominant intellectual tradition of the West, which always disdained "feeling" in favor of "reason."

Ever since Plato, one figure after another in the great line of Western philosophers has shown a pronounced distrust of emotion. According to the longest-reigning Western idea of reason and rationality, to be rational is to be "objective," which, in turn, is commonly taken to mean completely void of emotion. Mr. Spock of *Star Trek* is a popular recent image of the same idea, the idea that to be "logical" is to put all "feelings" out of play in making decisions.

I was brought up reading Plato and the other great Western thinkers, the great philosophers. Perhaps I caught philosophy from

WESTERN INTELLECTUAL BIAS AGAINST EMOTION

For the last twenty-five hundred years, beginning especially with Plato, the dominant Western intellectual tradition has shown a strong bias against the emotions, an "anti-emotionalism," in effect. Plato drew a sharp distinction between reason and emotion, then insisted that the emotions should always take a back seat to emotionless reason. That has remained the prevailing view in mainstream Western society to this day.

them (as one might catch the flu, or an infectious laugh). At any rate, while I was still in high school I decided I wanted to become a philosopher myself.

Soon enough, I did become one. At least I make my living from philosophy. I have taught it to university students for more than a quarter of a century now, for pay (something at which Plato, or at least his teacher Socrates, might well have frowned).

That's one reason I was still an emotional illiterate at forty: I'm a philosophy professor.

> touch me with noble anger,
> And let not women's weapons, water drops,
> Stain my man's cheeks!
>
> – SHAKESPEARE, *King Lear*

Another reason I was still an emotional illiterate at forty is that I'm also a man. That is, I am a *male* human being.

Women in our society can certainly be emotionally illiterate too. Like men, few women ever get more than the most rudimentary emotional education.

Nevertheless, the problem of extreme emotional illiteracy, in which even the most elementary emotional education is lacking, is especially severe among men in our society, because of the reigning cultural models of maleness and masculinity. Those models are all but universally encoded into male children from the moment of birth (if not even before that, given modern technologies that allow the sex of the fetus to be determined well before the child is born).

In our society men are traditionally discouraged from crying or otherwise directly displaying many of their feelings, talking much about how they feel, or in most other ways letting on that they even have emotions. From an early age, they are encouraged to "be a man" and not to display emotion. In one way or another, they are told that to display most emotions is a sign of weakness, and that men are supposed to be strong. Thus, they come to identify displaying emotion, or even being especially concerned about how they feel, with showing weakness. "Real men" don't do such things.

MEN AND EMOTION IN WESTERN SOCIETY

Men raised in the West are brought up to believe in the myth that "real men" don't feel emotions. Because Western men are discouraged from even admitting that they feel emotions, let alone talking about their emotions with others, as a class men in Western society suffer from an even higher degree of emotional illiteracy than do women.

However, there is one major exception to the rule that men are not to show emotions. That exception is anger. In general in our society, men are taught that it is often quite all right to display anger. In fact, by images in the mass media as well as by examples at home and in the local community, men are often given the impression that it is all right to show anger *most* of the time. Displaying anger is often represented as a sign of strength rather than weakness. When a man gets angry it is often taken to show pride, willingness to stand up for his "rights," and commitment to protecting "his" family and property, all three of which are perceived as "manly" virtues. "Real men" may not cry, but they are permitted, and often even encouraged, to "get mad."

Thus, it is not taken to be "unmanly" for a man to show anger. It is all right for men to do so. It is permissible for them to show anger under a wide variety of basic activities: when they are at home, when they are behind the wheel of a car, when they are at work, or when they are at play (especially when they are doing either of the last two, working or playing). Men are encouraged to be "competitive" and are praised for competing "aggressively": that just shows how strongly motivated they are.

Men brought up with such models tend to develop without much experience of acknowledging, expressing, and discussing their feelings, except for anger. As a result, they commonly have two interconnected difficulties when it comes to emotional education. First, such men often have a diminished capacity to tell the difference between their varied emotions and, accordingly, what those varied emotions reveal to them about themselves and their experience of their world. Since anger is the only emotion with which they have been allowed to experiment freely, they easily confuse other emotions with anger. They are tempted to interpret any perceived distress in themselves as a sign that they are angry at someone for some reason. Yielding to that temptation, they then look around to see who it is that has "made" them angry; then they act out their supposed anger on the person unfortunate enough to be selected.

More than one instance of domestic violence has no doubt occurred in that way. For example, a husband may experience a distressful emotion toward his wife. Perhaps what is involved is fear at the prospect of her abandoning him for another man, a fear that might have been brought on by him merely imagining his wife leaving him, even if she has done nothing to indicate such an intention. Having no experience at dealing with such emotions, or even with properly identifying them, he then confuses being frightened by the thought of his wife leaving him with being angry at her for something she has done. Having further been brought up to regard displaying anger as "manly" and having learned no other way to express anger than by acting it out through violence, he then abuses her.

The second difficulty men in our society commonly face in learning how to feel is closely tied to the first. It is a dangerously enlarged capacity to feel anger. Often, a man's capacity to grow angry becomes so enlarged that virtually anything happening to him that he doesn't want to happen, or even just not happening exactly the *way* he wants it to happen, can set him off into a rage.

Women have served all these centuries as looking-glasses possessing the magic and delicious power of reflecting the figure of man at twice its natural size. — Virginia Woolf, *A Room of One's Own*

Women in our society have to face their own set of common obstacles to emotional education. Although I am a man and fit the above pattern for men, suffering from both of the impairments common to men, I also suffer from two other impairments that seem, judging from what I have heard and read, to be more common among women than among men, at least in our society. Those two additional impairments have also made crucial contributions toward keeping me in emotional ignorance for so long.

The first of those two difficulties is an imbalance between attentiveness to the emotions of others, on the one hand, and attentiveness to my own emotions, on the other. Like many women, I often pay more attention to the emotional responses of the people around me than I do to my own.

For example, I am often more sensitive to my young daughter's moods than I am to my own. When she is around me, I often pick up even slight signals from her behavior, gestures, facial expression, and body language, signals that I read for information about how she is feeling from moment to moment. At such times, if someone were to ask me how my daughter is feeling, I would be able to answer with far more accuracy than I could if I were asked how I was feeling myself.

I am similarly often more aware of my wife's moods than I am of my own.

What accounts for my high sensitivity to their moods, coupled with a correspondingly low sensitivity to my own, is that I am emotionally dependent on both my daughter and my wife. The perceived threat of either of them abandoning me, even if "only" emotionally and not also physically, causes me severe agitation. Unconsciously (sometimes even quite consciously), I monitor their demeanor and behavior for warning signs of discontent. If I spot any, I try to protect myself from possible loss by adjusting my own behavior to fit my projection of how they "want" me to behave. Reading their perceived discontent as directed at me, I attempt to placate them, so they won't abandon me.

Another thing I do — which points to the second disability I seem to share with more women than men in our society — is that I often deflect anger I feel toward someone on whom I am emotionally dependent, such as my wife or daughter, away from that person and onto some third person. I take my anger out on others rather than risk offending those on whom I feel dependent. I do it unconsciously, so that I really don't even fully know myself that it is really my wife or daughter or the equivalent toward whom I feel anger. Instead, I somehow manage to convince myself that my anger is brought on by something some other person in my vicinity happens to have done. If asked why I am angry, I will answer — honestly but mistakenly believing it myself — that I am angry because of what that third party has done.

Thus, I suffer from a diminished capacity to recognize at whom my own feelings of anger are actually directed. If I feel anger toward any other person about whom I care, I have difficulty recognizing it. I tend to misunderstand the direction of my own anger and take it to be directed elsewhere than it actually is. For example, if I am angry at a colleague whose perceived good opinion of me is nevertheless important to my self-esteem, I will tend to act my anger out on someone else. I will take my anger out on that other person, convincing myself that I have really been angry at that third party all along.

A family's collective character may be clear to the outside world and discernible as a "corporate characteristic. . . . " A corporate characteristic is a family's public face; its myth is its inner image of itself.

— JUDITH VIORST, *Necessary Losses*

Yet another reason I turned forty before I began learning how to feel is that I come from what today is popularly called a dysfunctional family. Unfortunately for the aggressively competitive "masculine" part of me, I cannot claim that my family was more dysfunctional than average. The degree of dysfunction in my family may very well have been below average, in fact. But it was still dysfunctional enough to contribute significantly to my emotional illiteracy.

Like other dysfunctional families, mine taught us children a great deal more about how *not* to feel than about how *to* feel. We were trained to believe in what is often, in the literature of dysfunctionality, called "the family myth." That is a distorted image the family projects of itself, not only to others but also among its own members. This distorted image is internalized by family members, then continually reproduced, and thereby reinforced, whenever they speak or even think about the family. Members of the family thus come to believe that this publicly projected image is the truth about the family, even though the reality of daily family life continually offers refuting evidence.

In general, the reality in dysfunctional families is one of ongoing conflict between family members. Typically there is recurrent or constant tension between the two parents or their substitutes, as well as between them and the children, and often between the children themselves. Overt outbreaks of the underlying tension and conflict may

DYSFUNCTIONAL FAMILIES AND
EMOTIONAL ILLITERACY

Dysfunctional families have a vested interest in preserving the emotional illiteracy of their members. Through such devices as the "family myth" dysfunctional families teach children to deny their own true emotions and those of other family members. Thus, not only are children kept emotionally illiterate in such families, but they are also made to feel that learning to acknowledge and express their real emotions is an act of betrayal of the family, something bad to be ashamed of rather than something desirable and deserving of praise.

remain primarily at the verbal level, or they may escalate into occasional or continuing physical and/or sexual abuse. The tension and conflict are never (or only rarely, and then under special circumstances that neutralize the possible practical effect) openly acknowledged, let alone discussed. They therefore remain unresolved.

Nevertheless, the family myth is that all the members of the family love one another, and that the family is a proverbially happy one. Family members learn from one another in their daily life together to internalize and project, not only to those outside the family, but also to one another and to themselves, this falsifying image. Whenever they speak aloud of the family, among themselves as well as to outsiders, they affirm it. In one way or another, they frequently tell each other that, despite arguments and disagreements that may arise between them (after all, they say, that happens in every family), they remain "one big happy family." The details of my own specific family situation and the particularities of our own family myth are not important. They fit the basic pattern and help explain my emotional illiteracy.

From working with addicts we have learned that they tend to be almost totally out of touch with their feelings.

— ANNE WILSON SCHAEF, *When Society Becomes an Addict*

In addition to being an academic philosopher, a male member of contemporary American society, and a product of a dysfunctional family, I am one more thing that helps explain that illiteracy. Addiction often occurs in dysfunctional families, and mine was no exception. I am also an alcoholic.

Active alcoholism or other addictions and emotional illiteracy reciprocally reinforce one another. Not knowing how to feel makes one more inclined toward addiction of one form or another, since drinking, drugging, or engaging in some other potentially addictive practice helps one to escape one's unruly, unnamed emotions. In turn, once an addiction is formed, engaging in the addictive practice helps insulate one from the need to learn how to feel, thus helping perpetuate one's illiteracy.

As is common among addicts, life in my dysfunctional "family of origin" had taught me to be suspicious of feelings in general. Thus, when I learned as a teenager that all it took to get rid of any disturbing feelings was to take a drink, that's just what I did whenever I felt much of anything, regardless of whether it was pleasant or unpleasant. If I felt happy, that was no less reason to drink than if I felt sad, and the boring state between, which I usually occupied, offered at least as much excuse.

By drinking I could change or escape my feelings, which is precisely what I had learned to do from my family — with the exception of one emotion. The exception, of course, was anger. Even that, however, had to be properly deflected. Otherwise, anger too had to be carefully kept at bay.

My mother and father had modeled the deflection of anger very effectively for me, each in a way appropriate to the specific sexual and gender role she or he had been trained to occupy by earlier generations of dysfunctional parents. We children followed their lead. In part we learned to deflect our anger toward our parents onto one another, in part to take it out on available passersby. However, we also learned to take it out on ourselves. Each of us chose his or her individual means for doing so, and alcohol — supplemented by tobacco and a few other promising objects of addiction — came to my aid in that capacity as well.

ADDICTION AND EMOTIONAL ILLITERACY

Addiction and emotional illiteracy mutually reinforce one another. Addiction offers temporary relief from the awkwardness, pain, and discomfort of not knowing how to acknowledge and express what one feels. However, the price paid for that temporary relief is that the underlying condition of emotional confusion actually grows worse, which, in turn, just adds incentive for sinking deeper into the addiction in order to escape.

To sum up, I was a contemporary Western male offspring of a dysfunctional family and an intellectual steeped in alcohol no less than in philosophy. With all those strikes against me the wonder is not that I turned forty without yet having learned how to feel. The wonder is that I *ever* began to learn.

Ironically, the same alcoholism that for many years had allowed me to continue in affective ignorance eventually proved to be my salvation, when, late in my fortieth year of life, I finally "bottomed out."

Since then I have not only been an alcoholic, but also an alcoholic "in recovery." Being an alcoholic in recovery means I am someone who used to seem (at least to myself) to be unable to live without alcohol, but who finally learned how to do so, and is grateful for the lesson.

Once we have progressed beyond a certain point in the process, we alcoholics "in recovery" no longer have a problem with alcohol. Nor need we have a problem with it again, so long as we continue to follow "a few simple rules," to borrow a phrase from the book *Alcoholics Anonymous* — commonly called AA's "Big Book" by those familiar with it, whether AA members or not.

On the other hand — and strange as this may seem to those who do not understand — once a psychic change has occurred, the very same person who seemed doomed, who had so many problems he despaired of ever solving them, suddenly finds himself easily able to control his desire for alcohol, the only effort necessary being that required to follow a few simple rules.

— WILLIAM D. SILKWORTH, M.D.
"The Doctor's Opinion," *Alcoholics Anonymous*

One of those simple rules is not to drink. As the only alcoholism counselor I ever consulted for my own case, on the only occasion I ever consulted her, said to me: "If you have a problem with alcohol, don't drink." To borrow another phrase from AA's Big Book, that is "simple, but not easy." At least it's not easy for an alcoholic.

One reason that particular rule — don't drink — is so difficult for us alcoholics is that we have trouble remembering it, especially when we most need it. Put us in places or situations where we're accustomed to drinking, and we tend to forget we're not supposed to drink. It's only after we've already begun to drink that we remember. By then, unfortunately, it's too late to do us much good any more.

If it's only by violating a rule that we can remember it, the rule isn't of much use to us. All we can do with it by then is use it to make ourselves feel guilty — which, to an alcoholic's mind when drinking, is a good reason to have another drink.

Our problem, then, is that it's precisely when we *don't* drink that we forget we don't *want* to drink. It's only when we drink that we remember we don't want to. Accordingly, for us alcoholics the process of recovery is in large part a matter of memory training and maintenance.

Regularly spending time with other recovering alcoholics helps in that regard, since that way we can keep reminding one another that we don't want to drink any more. But that alone is not enough, if for no other reason than that we're not always together. We have to learn a whole new way of living, designed, in effect, to keep us remembering we no longer want to drink.

Among the things that can make us forget is to let ourselves grow "hungry, angry, lonely, or tired." Sometimes recovering alcoholics will therefore recommend one another to "HALT" — that is, not to allow ourselves to grow any of the four things from which that acronym derives.

However, to tell an emotional illiterate such as I was when I first quit drinking that he was not to let himself grow hungry, angry, lonely, or tired is like telling a baby to take dictation: even to the extent I was able to understand the advice (a severely limited extent, in the first place), I didn't have the vaguest idea how to set about heeding it. Hunger, anger, loneliness, and tiredness — all seemed pretty much the same to me; and I typically took them all to be anger. As for not "letting" myself grow angry, I really couldn't begin to imagine what that might even *mean*. So far as I had ever learned, my anger was under other people's control, not my own. (They were the ones who "made" me angry by refusing to do what I wanted them to do. Talk to *them* about not letting me get angry.)

In short, if I wanted to keep from forgetting, sooner or later, that I no longer wanted to drink, I had no choice: I had to start learning how to feel.

The following chapters contain the most important lessons I have learned since I began developing my own emotional literacy. Those lessons are framed by the story, told in my own way, of how I came to learn them myself. Throughout, I have sprinkled useful teaching aids: summaries, suggestions, quotations, advice. By reading my account of what I have learned and how I learned it, conjoined with using the

EMOTIONAL LITERACY AND
RECOVERY FROM ADDICTION

Recovering from addiction requires developing emotional literacy, "learning how to feel." But just as addiction and emotional illiteracy mutually reinforce one another, so do recovery and the development of emotional literacy. The further one goes in recovery, the more one learns how to feel; and the more one learns how to feel, the more progress one makes in recovery.

aids I offer along the way, the reader, too, can develop her or his own emotional literacy, learning how to feel.

"Learning how to feel." That phrase means two different but related things at once. First, it means learning *what that is — to feel*.

In my own case, with the possible exception of anger, until I was in my forties I never knew much about that, about what it meant to "feel" something. Throughout most of my life up to that point, whenever such a disturbing thing as a feeling began to surface on me, I tried to escape it as soon as possible. (Once I discovered alcohol, that was as soon as I could get a drink, of course.) I didn't really even know what "feelings" *were*.

In part, learning how to feel is, therefore, like learning how to drive. Both are matters of acquiring and developing new skills. Learning how to feel is developing the skill to feel something — anything, at first, then, gradually, the whole range of human emotions. Ever since I stopped drinking, I have been learning more and more about how to feel in that basic sense, the sense of learning *to* feel in the first place.

At the same time, when I finally gave up alcohol I also had to begin learning how to feel in another sense as well, the second of the two senses of the phrase. That is the sense of learning *which* feelings to

WHAT IT MEANS TO LEARN HOW TO FEEL

Becoming emotionally literate is learning how to feel, and that involves learning two interrelated things.

- Learning to feel in the first place: developing the capacity to feel the full range of human emotions, to feel all the emotions freely and deeply; and

- Learning what to feel: developing emotional responses that are appropriate to the actual situation at the time, both appropriate in kind and appropriate in intensity.

feel, in effect. That is, I had to begin learning which feelings went with which situations.

All I'd learned up to that point was that anger went with almost any situation. I had to unlearn that lesson and begin to learn other emotions and how they fit with things that happened to me. When someone gave me something, for example, if I wasn't going to feel angry at the giver (maybe for putting me under a perceived obligation to give something in return), just what was I to feel? What about all the other confusing situations that came my way? What was I to feel for each of them if it wasn't anger? I didn't know. I had to learn.

The chapters that follow tell what I learned, and try to teach it.

Self-Evaluation

Assess your own degree of emotional illiteracy. First, ask yourself the following questions.

- Was I raised in a Western culture?

- Am I college educated?

- Am I a man?

- Am I emotionally dependent on someone else (either one individual or a family or other group of individuals)?

- Am I the product of a dysfunctional family?

- Am I currently actively addicted to alcohol or drugs (or food, or relationships, or whatever)?

If you answer yes to any one of those questions, then you are definitely at risk for emotional illiteracy. The more affirmative answers, the greater the risk.

- At any given time, how aware are you of your own feelings? If you are often unaware of just what you are feeling, that is a strong indication that you are in need of basic emotional education. That is also true if you tend to be more sensitive to the feelings of others — particularly the feelings of others who are important to you — than you are to your own.

    Especially if you're a man, but also for women, reflect on your driving behavior. When you're driving on the highway, particularly in heavy traffic, do you tend to drive aggressively? Do you become tense and impatient? Do you scream at other drivers, or carry on an angry running commentary on their driving as you go along? If someone cuts you off in traffic, how do you respond? Do you let it go easily, or do you retaliate in some fashion (honking your horn, flashing your lights, making gestures, yelling, etc.)? Repressed or deflected anger has a way of bubbling out for many people whenever they get behind the wheel of a car. If that is true for you, it is all but certain you need help to develop your emotional literacy.

Disciplines, Practices, Exercises

Here are two simple exercises that anyone can do profitably. The first is meant to be practiced as a regular discipline. The second is designed to help you begin learning how to deal with any specific emotion when it starts to cause you difficulty in your life.

1. Begin keeping a daily "emotions log," a written record of your feelings. Keep the log simple. First, give a brief description of the situation (for example, "Regular department meeting at the office. John criticized my work, saying it was 'sloppy'"). Then describe what you felt in that situation (to stick with the same example, John's comment about your work, perhaps you'd record, "Anger, followed almost immediately by a sense of guilt and shame, which then gave way to a depressed feeling"). Especially when you begin keeping an emotions log, it is advisable to include it on your daily schedule. For many persons, the following schedule would be good: midmorning, lunch, midafternoon, and once in the evening. Stick with the practice. If you miss making an entry, don't use that as an excuse to stop. Just keep your schedule for the next entry. Be honest and record whatever you remember feeling, which at first may often be little or nothing. As you continue the practice over time, you will find not only that you become more sensitive to your emotions, but that your emotional life itself will begin to change and grow.

2. Whenever you find that some specific emotion is causing you difficulty (say anger), simply begin *counting* that emotion. That is, simply record — on a scratch pad in your purse, a scrap of paper in your wallet, or whatever else you can keep conveniently and reliably handy — how often you feel that emotion during the day. Once again, it is best to keep count according to a fixed schedule. Keep mental track of the count between scheduled times for recording. Just record the number of times you felt the emotion; then tally the sum at the end of each day. Don't make any special effort to control the emotion, to feel it less (or more) often. Just keep track of how often you actually do experience it. Furthermore, don't waste time worrying about whether what you felt was really the emotion in question and not some other emotion ("Was that anger, or was it fear?"), or whether you felt

it intensely enough to be worth counting ("Did I really feel irritation just now, or am I just imagining I did, so I can count something?"). The rule to follow is this: when in doubt about it, count it. Try this exercise and stick to it for at least one week; then reflect on what it teaches you (we'll return to that question in a later chapter).

– Two –

The Ethics of Anger

We are not called good or bad on the basis of our emotions.
— ARISTOTLE, *Nichomachean Ethics*

Not long ago, I participated in a series of three discussions at the local Episcopal church where I was then a member. The issue we were addressing was one that has recently troubled American congregations in almost every denomination. It is the issue of the place of gays and lesbians within the church community.

By order of our bishop and in preparation for our upcoming national convention, all congregations within the diocese were supposed to discuss two specific questions. The first was whether the Episcopal church should bless same-sex unions, as it does traditional heterosexual marriages. The second was whether practicing gays and lesbians should be eligible for ordination as priests and deacons in the Episcopal church.

To provide background and a common basis for discussion, the diocese had sent each congregation a three-part videotape. As directed by the diocese, we started each meeting by watching one part of the tape. Accordingly, we began our third and final meeting with the corresponding segment of the tape. That segment ended with a series of three interviews. All were with active Episcopalians from congregations within the diocese.

The first interview was with the parents of an adult gay son. They talked about how difficult it had been for them when their son had "come out." They told us how hard they had struggled to understand and support their son in his resolution to live an openly gay life. They went on to tell us that in their experience the church had been less

34

than helpful to them and their son. In fact, they said they had en-countered mostly coldness and hostility from that quarter. Though they spoke calmly and openly, their anger, as well as their pain, came across clearly.

In the second interview, an active and involved member of an-other congregation who was openly lesbian spoke of the difficulties she had encountered. She told how she experienced an ongoing strug-gle to maintain her personal integrity as both a lesbian and an active, committed church member. She, too, conveyed her underlying anger.

The final interviewee was a gay man who belonged to yet another congregation within the diocese. He said that he had learned to ac-cept the fact that he was gay, but that along the way he had also become convinced that homosexual acts themselves were sinful. He told us that he was attempting to "recover" from his once active homo-sexuality, and he spoke warmly of the support and encouragement his congregation had given him in his efforts.

After the tape ended, the priest chairing our meeting directed us to begin our discussion by sharing only the *feelings* we had from watching the tape. He asked us to confine ourselves to sharing with the group how watching it had actually made us feel, but not yet to express any personal opinions about anything we'd heard or seen. He encouraged us not to judge our own emotional responses either. There was never any "right" or "wrong" way to feel, he said. We just had whatever feelings we had, that was all.

The first congregant to speak was a man. I'll call him Chuck (not his real name).

Chuck mentioned the anger we'd heard expressed in the first two interviews, and then said that he felt angry too. He was angry because what the interviewees had said implied that he, Chuck, was himself bigoted, intolerant, prejudiced, and ignorant. According to Chuck, he was, by implication, being called all of those things simply because of the view he held about homosexuality — the view, namely, that homosexuality was a sin condemned repeatedly in the Bible and no more to be countenanced by the church than adultery or any other sin.

In effect, Chuck was angry at the interviewees for being angry at him (or people like him). In contrast, the interviewees had not made *me* angry. However, what Chuck had said did. As he spoke, I felt my anger rising. Following the lead of the first two interviewees — and on their behalf, as it were — I was angry at Chuck.

First, the interviewees were angry at Chuck (or those like him). Next, Chuck was angry back at them for being angry at him. In turn, I was angry back at Chuck, on the interviewees' behalf, for being angry back at them for being angry at him.

But if the priest who presided over our church discussion was right, when he told us that no emotion is either the "right" way to feel or the "wrong" way, then wasn't there something, paradoxically, wrong with Chuck's anger? For Chuck to be angry at the interviewees because they were angry at him or his like made sense only if there was something "wrong" about them being angry at him in the first place. If there was nothing wrong about their initial anger at him, then what right did Chuck himself have to grow angry at their anger? Chuck's own anger implied that there *was* a difference between "right" emotions and "wrong" ones.

Indeed, part of my own anger back at Chuck (for being angry at the interviewees for being angry at him) was for that very reason: it seemed to me that Chuck had broken the rules of the discussion, the rules the priest had just explained. The priest had told us not to *judge* our own or each others emotions, but only to accept both as expressions of how each of us actually felt. But by growing angry at the interviewees because of *their* anger, Chuck, it seemed to me, had violated that rule. As I understood the rule, Chuck was not supposed to *respond* to the emotions of others, including the interviewees. He was supposed to stick to his own feelings, and grant the rest of us, including the interviewees, the right to ours, whatever they might be.

On the other hand, if there was never anything right or wrong about how someone happened to feel, wasn't my own anger at Chuck just as much a violation of the rule as was his anger at the inter-

LOVING YOU FOR LOVING ME:
EMOTIONS AT TWO REMOVES

Our emotions are often our most direct response to our concrete situation. But often they are also our response to how we think others are emotionally responding to that same situation: my emotions become a response to what I perceive to be your emotions. Since the emotions in the two cases "feel" the same, it is easy to confuse them. Only an honest self-evaluation in each case can tell the difference. You need to ask yourself: Am I feeling the way I do because of how I perceive this situation myself, directly? Or am I feeling this way because of how I think you are feeling about this situation? For example: Do I really love you, or only your loving me (or at least what I take to be your loving me)?

viewees? After all, if everyone has a right to feel whatever she or he happens actually to feel on any given occasion, then Chuck must have had a right to feel his own anger. So I must have been wrong to feel anger at Chuck for being angry at the interviewees' anger at him. But then *my* feeling of anger was "wrong," which would again mean that there *is* a difference between "right" and "wrong" emotions. Thus, if the priest was right, both Chuck and I were wrong to feel anger, which is what we did feel. But if we were both wrong to feel what we did feel, then the priest was *not* right. If he was right, we were wrong; but if we were wrong, he wasn't right.

A very confusing situation (but not at all an uncommon one). To remove the confusion, I must make use of some basic distinctions pertinent to what I call the "ethics" of the emotions.

They are thought to be fools who fail to become angry at those matters
they ought, or in the way or when or at whom they ought.

— ARISTOTLE, *Nichomachean Ethics*

The first distinction is between two different senses in which I can speak of the "rightness" or "wrongness" of an emotion. In *one* sense, what the priest at my church said is correct: no emotion is either "right" or "wrong"; it's just "how one feels." In *another* sense, however, a given emotion can sometimes be the "right" way to feel, sometimes the "wrong" way to feel. I have to be careful to pay attention to just *which* of those two very different senses of "right" and "wrong" is at issue whenever I actually think about "rightness" and "wrongness" in the emotions. I will explain each sense in turn.

Our priest, to be sure, was certainly trying to express something important, when he said that there is no right or wrong about emotions. I have heard or read many other people say much the same thing. In fact, I would say the idea that there is nothing either right or wrong about any feeling has become part of popular folk psychology.

What such remarks are meant to express, I think, is in large part the same thing Aristotle already said many centuries ago. According to Aristotle in his *Nichomachean Ethics*, a person is neither to be praised nor blamed merely for the fact that she or he feels a given emotion on a given occasion. Thus, the fact that I felt anger at Chuck, or that he felt anger at the interviewees, or that they initially felt anger at him or his like, is not, of itself, anything for which any of us were to be blamed, nor anything for which we were to be praised. None of us was either a "bad" or a "good" person for feeling the anger each actually felt. I wasn't being "bad" when I felt anger at Chuck; he wasn't being "bad" when he felt anger at the interviewees; they were not being "bad" to feel their anger toward him in the first place. Nor were any of us being "good" by feeling anger.

I should not blame or praise anyone just for having or failing to have any given feeling in any given situation. I should accuse no one of wrongdoing (or rightdoing) just for feeling any certain way. As Aristotle goes on to observe, it is only if the way a person feels points to some underlying disposition or inclination that the person has actually cultivated (or failed to cultivate) that it would make sense to either praise or blame that person on the basis of having felt a certain way in a certain situation. To use his way of putting it, to praise or blame the person for feeling a certain way in a given situation would make sense only if feeling that way in that situation revealed something about the person's underlying "character."

Another way of putting the general idea is that there is nothing *morally either right or wrong about any given feeling in any given situation. I know nothing of a person's "morals" or lack of morals, if all I know is how that person happens to feel* at a given moment.

Thus, emotions cannot be said to be either "right" or "wrong" in the *moral* sense of those terms. However, that doesn't mean there is no other important sense in which they can be said to be right or wrong.

To continue with the example of anger, I have had a lot of personal experience in dealing with anger that was somehow "wrong," even if not morally wrong. From the very beginning of my recovery from alcoholism I have had to deal with a great amount of such anger in myself.

In my years of drinking, very often the smallest things would set off attacks of strong anger in me, if not outright rage. At such times the intensity of my anger would be way out of proportion to the importance of the incidents that set them off. Or so it invariably seemed to those at whom my anger was directed. Even those who might simply be with me at such times, without themselves being the focus of my anger, often told me later that my anger had been out of proportion. In fact, I often saw it that way myself, once I calmed down. Sometimes I would then go so far as to apologize to whomever I'd been angry at, and perhaps try to excuse my behavior by saying I must have been overtired, or that I'd been worried about something unrelated that had made me edgy, or maybe even that I just didn't know "what came over me."

To the extent that the anger I felt on such occasions was way out of proportion to what occasioned it, my anger didn't "make sense." In that sense, I "shouldn't" have felt it. I "should" have felt less anger, or no anger at all.

When I felt anger out of proportion to the situation, I wasn't being "bad." I wasn't misbehaving or committing some morally questionable act by feeling the way I felt. There was nothing wrong (or right) about my anger at all, in *that* sense. Rather, there was something wrong about the way I *felt:* My frequently feeling such intense anger indicated that I was suffering from a sort of affective malady — some sort of illness of feeling itself. It showed that I needed to be restored to better emotional health or balance.

To give an analogy, sometimes when I start up my car it makes an unusual noise. When that happens, sometimes I say to myself that the car "shouldn't" sound that way, that there is something "wrong" about the way it sounds. But of course that doesn't mean that I am accusing my car of some reprehensible conduct. It's not as if my car deserves to be punished for making such a noise, or as if it needs to be disciplined not to make such noises in the future. What it means is that the car may need to be checked for a possible mechanical problem, something requiring repair.

In the same way, when I feel the "wrong" thing, that just means that my feeling indicates I may need some emotional repair, in effect. *Morally,* there's nothing either right or wrong about feeling any given way in any given situation, any more than there is with my car making a strange noise when I start it up. There's nothing either praiseworthy or blameworthy about feeling one way rather than another. But just as the strange noise alerts me to a possible mechanical problem in my car, so does my situationally wrong or inappropriate emotion alert me to a possible *emotional* or *affective* problem in myself.

To give another example, if a caring, knowing friend tells a battered woman that she "shouldn't" feel ashamed and guilty for the beating she has received, the friend is not accusing the battered woman of misbehaving. The woman has not "done anything wrong," and by telling her that she "shouldn't" feel guilt the friend is hardly suggesting that the woman feel even more guilt — namely, additional guilt about having felt guilty for being beaten in the first place. Rather, the

SITUATIONAL FIT (I): IS THE EMOTION IN PROPORTION?

Emotions can fail to "fit" the situation in which they occur. This can take one of two forms. The first way in
which emotions can fail to fit the situation is by being
out of proportion. A minor inconvenience may set off a
rage, for example; or, on the other hand, some major offense may trigger no more than a slight irritation. In the
first case, in proportion to what occasions it the anger is
too much; in the second case, it is too little. In either
case, what is out of place is the *amount* or *intensity* of the
emotion. Whenever my emotions are out of proportion
in either direction — too much or too little — it is a tip-
off that what needs attending to is more myself than the
situation.

effect is exactly the opposite. It is to assure the woman that indeed
she has *not* done anything wrong and that the very fact she feels she
has is itself just one more indication that she has been abused.

That any woman would feel shame and guilt for being beaten by
a man is itself demonstration that she has been abused. It shows that
she has been abused not only physically, but also emotionally, by being made to feel that her suffering was deserved, that she somehow
brought it on herself. Feelings of shame and guilt in such circumstances indicate that those who have such feelings need emotional
care, just as the strange noise my car sometimes makes may show
that it needs repair. (Beyond that point, of course, the analogy between a battered woman and a car breaks down. A woman is not
some sort of machine that needs regular tune-ups, occasional parts-
replacements, and sometimes major rebuilding. A battered woman
needs to be restored to full physical and emotional health, not just
"fixed" or "repaired" as though she were a machine.)

The persistently recurrent, intense anger I used to feel over minor things was a sign that something was emotionally wrong with me, just as similar feelings toward his wife that might incline some abusive husband to beat her would indicate something emotionally wrong in him. In contrast, it is not because she feels anger toward her batterer that there is something wrong in a battered woman. Instead, it is because she does *not* show anger, but shows shame and guilt instead. In her case, anger would be quite appropriate; it is the batterer who should feel the shame and guilt.

It is a spiritual axiom that every time we are disturbed, no matter what the cause, there is something wrong with us.
                                        – AA's *Twelve Steps and Twelve Traditions*

The observation that the batterer is the one who should feel the shame leads me to the second basic distinction that needs to be made in discussions of the ethics of the emotions. That is the distinction between cases in which having a given emotion in a given situation tells me that there is something that requires attention *in the situation,* and cases in which it tells me that there is something that requires attention *in me.*

This second distinction follows from the first. The fact that I feel a situationally inappropriate feeling — that I have the "wrong" feeling for that particular situation — tells me something about *myself.* It tells me that *I* need attention. On the other hand, if I have the "right" feeling for the given situation, then my feeling is telling me to attend to something in the situation itself, not in myself.

With regard to anger, when I feel angry do I need to respond by trying to do something about the situation in which I find myself? Should I, perhaps, take action against someone or something, or at least verbally express my anger to someone about something? That would be the case only if anger is the right feeling to have in that situation.

Or should I respond to my anger by trying to do something about myself rather than my situation? Should I, perhaps, seek therapeutic

SITUATIONAL FIT (II): IS THE EMOTION APPROPRIATE TO THE SITUATION?

A second way that emotions can fail to "fit" the situation is by being inappropriate, the "wrong" emotion for the situation in question. For example, a wife may feel shame for being abused by her husband — a situation in which anger toward the abuser would be the healthy, appropriate emotion. As with the first way in which emotions can fail to fit the situation (by being out of proportion), when my emotions are inappropriate, they indicate that something needs attention in me. However, at the same time inappropriate emotions are a tip-off that there is also something wrong in the situation itself. In fact, what makes an emotion situationally inappropriate in the first place is precisely this: my inappropriate emotions mask or disguise what is unacceptable in my situation, making it look as if I am what needs changing, when what really needs changing is the situation. The abused wife doesn't need to make herself even more compliant and "obedient," as her inappropriate emotion of shame tells her; she needs to leave the abusive relationship, just as the anger she "should" feel would indicate to her, if her shame did not block it. In that situation, her anger toward the abuser would serve the wife herself, whereas her shame toward herself ends up serving her husband, the abuser.

---

help or join some support group, or at least reflect calmly on what my anger tells me about my own emotional condition? If anger is the wrong feeling for the situation in which I find myself, then such efforts directed toward examining and possibly changing myself are precisely what is called for.

To escape looking at the wrongs we have done another, we resentfully focus on the wrong he has done us.

— AA's *Twelve Steps and Twelve Traditions*

To return to the discussion at my church, for which of us — the interviewees, Chuck, or myself — was anger the situationally right or appropriate way to feel? Was the anger of the interviewees who thought they had been victims of homophobia appropriate? What about Chuck's anger at them in return? What about my own anger at Chuck's angry response to their anger?

Were we all equally justified (or equally unjustified) in feeling anger? Or was anger justified only for some of us, not for others? What was the anger actually telling us in each case? What sort of response or responses did the feeling of anger call for in each oc-currence? Did it point to something wrong in the external situation, something that called for action to right it? Action to remedy an in-justice, perhaps? Or did it point to something wrong in those of us who felt the anger and call, accordingly, for action to right ourselves, to restore ourselves to emotional balance or health?

To answer such questions I need to introduce yet another distinc-tion, this time between what I call "the anger of indignation" and what I call "the anger of defensiveness." The anger of indignation is what I feel when I perceive something as an *injustice,* either against myself or against some other person, even if I have no personal con-nection to that other person. The anger of defensiveness, in contrast, is what I feel when I perceive myself or some other person with whom I do have a personal connection to be *threatened* by something.

The anger of indignation is an immediate or underived emotional response to a situation of a certain type. By that I mean that it is not what might be called a "second-order" emotional response — a response not directly to the perceived situation, but rather a response to an earlier emotional response that has already been called up by that same situation. A simple example will show what I mean.

If someone plays a practical joke on me by hiding in a darkened room, then jumping out at me and hollering "Boo!" when I enter, my *first* emotional response is likely to be *fear*. No sooner have I discovered that the whole thing is a joke, however, than my fear may be replaced by *anger* — anger at the practical joker *for* frightening me. The fear is my immediate, direct emotional response to the situation; the anger that soon replaces it is more a response to the fear I first feel, and only through that does it relate to the situation.

I call such anger "the anger of defensiveness," or "defensive anger," because it arises from the perception of a situation as threatening to me in some way and because it serves the effort to defend myself against the perceived threat. In effect, such anger belongs to the "fight" half of the "flight or fight" response triggered by *fear*. It *masks* fear, in effect, by putting a fierce face on that fear.

The anger of those who were interviewed on the tape, those in the first two interviews who thought they had been victimized by a homophobic church, was the anger of indignation. As such, it was appropriate to the situation, at least as the interviewees honestly perceived it. They felt anger at people like Chuck because they thought his views were unfair to gays and lesbians. They were in the same position as a woman who feels anger toward her husband because she honestly thinks he has abused her.

In contrast, Chuck's anger was the anger of defensiveness. It was the kind of anger someone who perceives his position to be threatened might feel. As the feminist philosopher Elizabeth Spelman has pointed out, when I think myself to be in a position of power or authority over others, if those others display anger at me for something I do or say to them, I tend to experience their anger as a threat to my position. I perceive their anger itself as a form of *insubordination*. As I see it, they are "getting out of line," "forgetting their proper place," being "uppity," or the like. It is the sort of anger an abusive husband might use to excuse abusing his wife for such "provocation" as not having dinner ready when he expects it.

Defensive anger often flares in an inflated ego quick to take offense. That was how I perceived Chuck's anger toward the interviewees: as

---

ANGER AT INJUSTICE VS.
ANGER AS INJUSTICE

The anger of indignation is the anger we feel when we experience a wrong done to ourselves or when we see or hear
of a wrong done to others. It is our spontaneous rebellion
against injustice. On the other hand, when we feel the
anger of defensiveness, it is we who are perpetrating the
wrong. In the anger of defensiveness, we are attempting to
assert our own power over others. The anger of defensiveness is a reaction against not having our own way, like a
spoiled child throwing a temper tantrum.

---

the anger of bruised pride. It seemed to me that Chuck had then acted
out his defensive anger by accusing the *interviewees* of an injustice
toward *him* — an injustice supposedly perpetrated by the mere fact
that they had dared to express anger toward those who held views in
agreement with Chuck's views.

By leveling such an accusation, however, Chuck had only *compounded* the injustice toward the interviewees. In his accusations he
had tried to put *them* on trial, as it were — on trial for having dared
to complain about what they had perceived as mistreatment in the
first place. Chuck's response to the interviewees added to the injustice
originally perpetrated against them because it denied them the right
even to protest against that initial perceived injustice.

The case is like that of a dysfunctional family in which the children
are abused, at least emotionally, if not also verbally or even physically/
sexually, and in which initial abuse is made all the more destructive
by the perpetration of a family myth in accordance with which everything in the family is fine. Members of the family continually tell
one another how "loving" the family is. Even in the face of their own
direct experience to the contrary, the children themselves eventually
internalize that myth. Once that has occurred, their own anger and

despair over their situation can appear to the children themselves only as proof of their own ingratitude. It shows them how "bad" they really are, and how, therefore, they "deserve" whatever ill treatment they receive. Often, of course, that message is verbally reiterated by the abusers themselves, who tell those they abuse, "You made me do it," or the equivalent. In that way the victims are made to accept blame for their own victimization.

Like Klansmen lynching blacks or Nazis murdering Jews, husbands who beat their wives and fathers who molest their children can be expert at using such devices to coerce their victims into participation in their own victimization. In denying victims even the right to voice anger about being victimized, victimizers doubly abuse them. In that way, victims are robbed of all sense of agency, and the hope that goes with it. All that is left to them is despair.

> "I'm mad as hell, and I'm not going to take it any more!"
> – PETER FINCH, in the movie *Network*

Thus, it is often a *positive* sign when victims come to feel and acknowledge anger toward their victimizers. Such anger is the victims' own emerging awareness of having been victimized. Becoming aware of being a victim, however, is a first, indispensable step toward ceasing to be one. It shows that those in bondage are already beginning to cast off their chains. That is why abusers take any display of anger toward them by those they abuse to be insubordination, as Elizabeth Spelman notes. Whatever offers hope to the oppressed is a threat to the oppressor.

To that degree, victims' anger at their victimizers is not only justifiable; it is desirable. It indicates a marshaling of the victims' resources toward overcoming their victimization. As moral theologian J. Giles Milhaven argues in his book *Good Anger*, anger asserts equality. It implicitly advances a claim of independence and personal agency. It says for the one feeling it: "I have a *right* to be angry at what has been done to me."

Those who maintain power over others only through force rather than through genuine authority are, therefore, correct to see their position threatened if their subjects begin to express anger toward them. It is threatening to the victimizers when the victims of injustice even dare to feel such anger, let alone when they dare to act upon it.

From the perspective of the oppressors, it is much better if those they oppress deflect their anger onto one another, thereby diverting it from its proper target, the oppressors themselves. Within African-American communities, black-on-black violence, especially among the black underclass, and rioting in which it is predominantly local neighborhoods and businesses that are damaged are examples of such deflection of legitimate anger over unacceptable conditions. So are the effects of addiction and the drug traffic that goes with it, which are particularly destructive within those same communities, as well as within other minority communities. As various African-American spokespersons have pointed out, it is no accident that concern about drugs and drug usage became a national priority only in the 1960s, when drugs began to move into the overwhelmingly white suburbs of the American middle class.

It is understandable when victims of oppression take out their anger over their condition on one another if they are denied the possibility of directing it toward their oppressors, where it belongs. It is understandable, but regrettable. It is also understandable, when oppressors grow angry toward those they oppress for expressing their own anger over oppression — especially if they express it directly to the oppressors themselves. It is understandable, but *reprehensible.*

What's wrong in the case of the anger of the oppressed is not that the oppressed grow angry about being oppressed. They should. What's wrong, rather, is that their anger becomes misdirected by being deflected onto one another rather than kept focused where it really belongs. The fact that the oppressed feel anger about being oppressed tells them that they need to do whatever they can to liberate, not to destroy, themselves. Their anger tells them that something is wrong, not in those who feel the anger — namely, the oppressed themselves — but in something that has been done to them. What needs changing is the world.

In contrast, what's wrong in the case of the anger of the oppressors is precisely the anger that the oppressors feel (the anger itself, by the way, not just their subsequent behavior in reaction to that anger). Oppressors shouldn't feel anger when those they oppress angrily protest against oppression. Instead, they should feel guilt — a guilt inviting them to cease acting oppressively. What's wrong in this second case is that the oppressors feel anger when they should feel guilt. Their anger tells the oppressors that what's wrong is in themselves. It is they who need changing, not the world.

Self-Evaluation

Take a good, hard look at your own anger. Do things that should make you angry actually do so? Do you get angry when you should, at the appropriate persons, and with the right intensity? Or are you one of those "fools" Aristotle mentions, who gets mad at the wrong times, toward the wrong people, to the wrong degree, for the wrong reasons? Here are four key questions to ask yourself that may help you find out:

- Do you easily get angry at others for being angry at you? If so, you are probably being defensive and need to work on growing in your understanding of, and empathy for, others.

- Do you tend to "fly off the handle"? Or, in contrast, do you tend to put up with things, no matter how bad, without complaint? Or do you tend to combine the two, putting up with things until you reach a boiling point, then exploding with anger? If any of the three fit you, then you are having problems with the proportion or intensity of your anger.

- Do you sometimes fault yourself for "letting your anger get the best of you"? This could also be a sign that you are having problems of proportion, but it might be a sign, on the other hand, that you need to do more of the very thing you are faulting yourself for doing: getting angry. To tell which is at issue for you, look at yourself in your concrete situation. Are you suppressing your anger toward someone or something? Or are you just indulging your self-righteousness?

- Do you sometimes feel ashamed right after you feel anger, regardless of the intensity of the feeling (even sometimes when it's only a mere trace of irritation, for example)? That is often a tip-off that you are caught in an abusive relationship or other situation that needs changing. At any rate, it is an indication that you need to look at the situational appropriateness of your emotions.

Make a thorough evaluation of your own anger. The above questions are just to get you started. Some of the exercises below may also be helpful to you. In general, as you take stock of yourself trust your own judgment about which exercises will be of most use to you, just as long as you remain committed to the basic task of taking an honest look at the place and role of anger in your own life.

Disciplines, Practices, Exercises

First, here are two applications of the basic exercises suggested at the end of chapter 1. They are designed to assist you in your self-evaluation of the place and role of anger in your own life.

1. Use the counting exercise suggested at the end of the last chapter, this time focusing exclusively on your anger. This exercise will help sensitize you to your own anger, especially to the frequency and intensity of the anger you experience in your daily life.

2. Keep an "anger log." Follow the instruction for the "emotions log" given at the end of chapter 1, but confine your attention to anger for the time being rather than keeping track of all your

emotions at once. After you've kept your anger log for a while —
a few days or a few weeks, whatever gives you enough material
for reflection — review it carefully. Be especially attentive to the
situations in which you feel anger. Look for situational "fit" or
"misfit" in both of the two senses explained in this chapter: proportion and appropriateness. The cases of "misfit" will tell you
the most about where you need to look deeper.

Next, here are two completely new exercises. They are designed to
let you experiment with increasing your own options in dealing with
anger. The first is an exercise in watchfulness; the second is an exercise
in choice.

3. On the basis of what you've learned about yourself and your
   anger from the preceding two exercises (counting your anger and
   keeping an anger log), begin paying particular attention to the
   onset of anger in you. That is, start trying to detect the first
   rumblings of anger, the initial signs that it is coming, its first
   glimmerings. Don't wait until the anger is fully upon you before you notice it. Instead, try to develop sensitivity to the early
   warning signs of impending anger.

4. Just as an experiment, if for no other reason, try this: as soon as
   you notice yourself beginning to grow angry — at the very first
   signs you notice of impending anger — try deliberately to choose
   not to be angry. Choose, that is, just to let the anger go. Don't
   worry about whether the anger is "justified" or not; just let it go,
   so far as you are able. Keep at this exercise, even if you find yourself growing discouraged at your initial inability to exercise any
   choice over your own anger. That is, keep at it even if you find (as
   most of us do) that you have very little "control" over your own
   anger. As with any exercise, you will find that the more you practice, the better you will get at it. In fact, that is really what this
   exercise is for: to build your capacity for *choosing* whether you are
   going to be angry or not. (Driving on downtown freeways during
   rush-hour is a great time to practice this exercise, by the way.)

– Three –

Beyond Anger

We must be free of anger. We must, or it kills us.
– Alcoholics Anonymous

In the Middle Ages anger was classified as one of the Seven Deadly Sins, and Christian admonitions to beware of anger and to rid oneself of it are as old as Christianity itself. The Jesus of the Gospels tells his disciples that, if they have any anger toward one of their brothers, they must first reconcile with him before they approach the altar to make an offering. In his letters Paul warns Christians not to let the sun set on their anger, and other authors in the Christian Scriptures sound the same theme. From then on, it recurs throughout the history of the literature of Christian spiritual direction.

The Dalai Lama, spiritual leader of all who follow Tibetan Buddhism, puts anger among the "negative" emotions that must be overcome before one can attain enlightenment. Thich Nhat Hanh, the Vietnamese Buddhist master living in exile since the Vietnam war, whom Martin Luther King, Jr., once nominated for the Nobel peace prize and who, like the Dalai Lama, has a worldwide following, delivers the same verdict on anger. The attitude of those two contemporary Buddhist leaders toward anger represents an entire Buddhist tradition, one even more ancient than Christianity.

Similar ideas can be found in other religious traditions, besides Christianity and Buddhism. The quotation from *Alcoholics Anonymous* illustrates that warnings against anger can also be found in contemporary "self-help" literature. Such admonitions often surface in other areas of contemporary popular culture as well (for example, television and radio talk-shows).

In that same popular culture, however, another current of thought about anger also repeatedly comes to expression, a current that, at least at first glance, seems to run in an opposite direction. That second current manifests itself in remarks such as that of the priest who presided over the church discussions I mentioned in the preceding chapter, who told my congregation, in effect, that feelings themselves were neither good nor bad, but were "just" feelings. It also surfaces in many works of popular psychology whenever readers are cautioned against "stuffing" their anger and are encouraged, instead, to express it. Psychiatrist Theodore Isaac Rubin's *The Angry Book*, first published in 1969, is one widely read example of a popular presentation of such a view.

Proponents of that view argue that it is unhealthy to "bottle up" one's anger. They encourage everyone to learn to vent their anger rather than to "hold it in." Such venting is not necessarily to take the form of acts of vengeance against those at whom one has come to feel anger. In fact, by learning how properly to admit and discharge one's anger, one can supposedly learn how to *avoid* acts of retaliatory vengeance directed against others.

Accordingly, a commonly recommended technique is to act one's anger out on a pillow rather than on the person toward whom one feels the anger. The idea is that I may be able to discharge my anger toward my wife, for example, by beating up my pillow instead of her.

Against that very technique, Thich Nhat Hanh comments that acting my anger out on my pillow is *not* to be encouraged. All that beating my pillow will accomplish, he says, is to make me angry at it too. Neither I nor my pillow really benefits at all.

Of course, if I have to beat up something, beating up my pillow is preferable to beating up my wife. But at most, according to Thich Nhat Hanh, what I will gain from such a substitution is only a temporary respite from the distress of feeling angry. If I beat my pillow vigorously enough, I will eventually tire myself out. As a result, exhaustion will replace anger for the time being. However, none of the underlying conditions that gave rise to my anger in the first place will have been affected in the least. Ideally, from Thich Nhat Hanh's perspective, I will beat up neither my wife nor my pillow. Nor will I find some third object with which to replace both. I will, instead, learn how to overcome anger itself. Ideally, I will eventually grow beyond anger altogether. That, according to Thich Nhat Hanh, is the goal I should set myself.

Through my own experience I know how easy it is to misunderstand such recommendations as Thich Nhat Hanh's or AA's Big Book — recommendations that I "free" myself from anger, grow "beyond" it. Like many alcoholics or other addicts in recovery, when I first encountered such ideas, I took them to mean that I was simply not "supposed" to feel anger at all; therefore, if I did, it meant I was "doing something wrong." That is, I took such ideas to be recommendations that I *control* my anger — that I "swear off" anger, as it were.

I took such ideas to heart, as I understood them. That is, I tried to swear off anger. I tried to control my temper. When I would feel my gorge begin to rise, I would force myself to swallow it back down and, instead, to "put on a happy face."

However, my attempt to swear off anger proved no more successful than my numerous attempts to swear off alcohol or cigarettes had ever been. For a while, I was indeed able to "catch" myself whenever I started to boil over, and I would turn off the heat. At least I would refrain from retaliating against anyone toward whom I began to feel heated. But sooner or later, I'd "slip" and lash out in anger, at least verbally attacking someone or something to vent my rage. If anything, my outbursts, when they did occur, were worse than ever, since they now added the force of numerous stifled past discontents to that of the present complaint, whatever that happened to be.

Thus, by trying valiantly to keep my own anger in check, I only succeeded is making it more of a problem than ever. According to the first of AA's Twelve Steps, as an alcoholic I was "powerless" over alcohol. My attempts to control my own anger proved to my own satisfaction that I was certainly powerless over anger.

REPRESSING, ENACTING, OR ACCEPTING
"NEGATIVE" EMOTIONS

To *repress* anger or any other distressing, so-called negative emotion is to try to "deny" it. When I repress an emotion I deny the emotion to *myself*, not just to others. In a paradoxical way, I don't let myself know what I know. Instead, I try to sweep my own emotions under the rug, as it were. I just hide them, without learning anything from them or doing anything to clean up whatever mess they make. Like dirt swept under a carpet, however, repressed emotions don't go away. When I sweep dirt under the carpet, it just keeps accumulating, making it all the harder to clean it up when the time eventually comes that I have to. The same applies to repressed emotions: repression doesn't make them go away; it just allows them to keep on growing.

To *enact* an emotion is to go ahead and do what the emotion itself invites or sets me up to do. Thus, to enact fear would be to run away from, or to fight against, whatever frightens me. To enact anger would be to strike out, physically or verbally, at whatever or whomever evokes my anger, "makes me mad." Enacting an emotion may succeed in eliminating the cause or reason for feeling the emotion in the first place: if I succeed in running away from something that frightens me, then my fear subsides, at least so long as I can continue to keep away from whatever I'm afraid of. However, precisely because it aims at eliminating the very emotion it enacts, enacting an emotion keeps me from learning whatever the emotion may have to tell me about myself and my world.

In contrast, by *accepting* the anger or other distressing emotion I allow myself to learn from it. Only by accepting the emotion, without trying either to deny it or to make it go away by enacting it, can I ever hope to grow beyond it.

When I first read such things as the passages about anger in AA's Big Book, I thought I was supposed to stop being angry, just like that. I thought I was supposed to be able to resolve to myself never to get angry again and then use my will power to keep that resolution.

What I failed to realize is that the only way I could keep such a resolution is if I really didn't *need* to keep it. If I had been capable of reigning my anger in by no more than my own choice, I would *already* have been "free" of anger. My failed efforts to do just that—give up my anger by simple choice—simply proved that the ideas in AA's Big Book applied to me: I was someone who was *not* free of anger and who needed to *get* free.

It was precisely my "slips" back into anger, despite all of my own best intentions and efforts, that eventually brought me to see that that was what passages such as those from AA's Big Book were really trying to tell me: that I was a slave of my own anger and that I needed to find some way to become free of it. I eventually realized that being free of anger did not so much mean never feeling anger. It meant, rather, being able really *to* feel it—to feel it fully and honestly rather than to repress and deny it—and then to learn from it what it had to teach me.

When I made vain attempts to control my own anger, I confused being free of anger with the denial of anger. That confusion saw to it that my efforts to free myself from anger would only entangle me in it all the more, as denial always makes any problem worse rather than better.

The denial of anger does not free me from anger. It does not go beyond anger. It falls short of it. It does not rise above anger, but stays submerged beneath it.

The way beyond anger does not go through denial. Instead, the full *acceptance* of one's own anger is the first and most crucial step toward genuinely rising above it. Denied, anger can never be transformed, but anger acknowledged lies open to the possibility of transformation. As acknowledging and accepting new responsibilities helps young people outgrow the irresponsibilities of adolescence, acknowledging and accepting anger helps me outgrow anger.

FREEDOM FROM ANGER

To be free of anger does not mean never to feel anger. It means, instead, to be free in relation to the very anger one does feel. Having freedom from anger is not the same as being "anger-free." To adapt a line from Aristotle, to be anger-free would be to be either a god or an inanimate object, but not a human being. Having freedom from anger is, rather, owning my own anger and no longer letting myself be owned by it. That is, when I am free of anger, then instead of letting my behavior be dictated to me by my anger, I maintain my liberty of choice about how I will respond to those situations in which I do feel anger.

By acknowledging heretofore repressed or denied anger, I begin to recover from anger as from an illness. I begin to overcome anger.

Overcoming an obstacle is not the same thing as avoiding it. Instead, to overcome an obstacle I must first *stop* avoiding it. I must stop denying it, and instead confront it.

If anger is an obstacle for me, then to overcome my anger I must first confront it. I must face my own anger rather than attempting to avoid or deny it.

> *Cherish your anger, like a baby.*
> – THICH NHAT HANH,
> "Buddhism and Psychotherapy"

When I first came to understand what being free of anger really meant and began to acknowledge my own anger in an effort to overcome it, for a while it actually seemed to me that I was only becoming angrier than ever. At the time, I had just come across St. Ignatius of Loyola's *Spiritual Exercises.* Ignatius was the founder of the Jesuits in the sixteenth century, and his book on how to make spiritual progress through following a regimen of reflective exercises coupled with continuing regular moral self-examination has been in wide usage, especially among Roman Catholics, ever since he wrote it.

From Ignatius I borrowed the useful technique of simply *keeping count* of the number of times each day one is troubled by some impulse about which one is especially concerned (the first exercise recommended at the end of chapter 1 in this book). I applied that to myself and my anger. I started monitoring my feelings, looking for flashes of anger, no matter how slight. Each time I felt a stab of anger or resentment — each time I began to take offense, for whatever reason, at something someone said or did, or failed to say or do, I made note of it, not only mentally but also by making a mark, as soon as practicable, on a tally sheet I carried in my wallet for that purpose.

After doing that for only a few hours, I was shocked at how many times anger had flared in me. It seemed that almost anything anyone ever said or did, or didn't say or do, was enough to elicit at least an initial stirring in me of anger. I wondered if I wasn't looking for extra excuses to feel anger, just so I could have something to count on my tally sheet, and if I wasn't thereby perhaps creating a problem where there had been none before.

Twentieth-century physics teaches that, especially at the subatomic level, the very effort to observe an event changes it. A similar phenomenon may well have occurred when I tried, following Ignatius's advice, to observe my own anger. Perhaps the very act of observing my anger increased it.

Be that as it may, however, there was surely also another factor in play, when my anger seemed to me actually to *increase* once I began attending to it. That other factor is the "pressure-cooker" effect: after being bottled up for so long, once the lid was finally lifted off all my pent-up anger of many years, it explosively bubbled to the surface. When I began to acknowledge my own anger after years of deflecting and denying it, I probably didn't really grow angrier than ever. It probably only seemed that way, because I was finally allowing myself to experience how angry I had been all along, but had managed to repress.

When I unsuccessfully tried to free myself from anger by simple will power, although in a sense I at least *acknowledged* my anger, I still did not fully *accept* it. In one sense, I had stopped denying it; but I still openly resisted it. I continued to reject it. (No longer *re*pressing it, I still *sup*pressed it.).

In effect, after acknowledging my own anger I tried to overcome it by attacking it. I grew angry at my own anger.

Thus, at that point (before I found Ignatius and others to help me) there actually *was* an increase in my anger. In addition to the anger I had been repressing for so long, as well as the deflected anger I had learned to allow myself to vent, there was now my newfound anger at my own anger. Seeking to outgrow anger, I achieved the very opposite: I grew angrier instead.

To escape that circle I had to stop being angry at my own anger, and at myself for not being able to control it. I had to learn, as Thich Nhat Hanh puts it, to "cherish" my own anger rather than to reject it angrily (he says I should cherish my anger "like a baby").

> To give your sheep or cow a large, spacious meadow is the way to control him. So it is with people: first let them do what they want, and watch them. This is the best policy. To ignore them is not good; that is the worst policy. The second worst is trying to control them. The best one is to watch them, just to watch them, without trying to control them. — Shunryu Suzuki, *Zen Mind, Beginner's Mind*

If I cherish something, I don't ignore it. I give it my full attention. When I give my anger full attention by fully accepting it, my anger itself is immediately calmed, at least to some extent, just as an angry child is already somewhat calmed just by the fact that its parents attend to its cries.

When another person toward whom I express displeasure acknowledges my anger and offers to discuss things with me, right away I begin to calm down. For that matter, it calms me even when a third party notices my anger and inquires solicitously about it. The same effect occurs to a surprising extent even when I genuinely pay attention to my own anger for myself.

To cherish my anger is to treat it with the same respect with which a solicitous third party might treat it. To cherish it, I must ask my anger about itself. I must give my anger a chance to tell me what's troubling it and listen attentively to what it says. After patiently hearing my anger out, I must then attentively consider my own options for responding to what it tells me, looking carefully for the best way to continue to be of help.

One of my options in the face of anger is to act the anger out. I may act it out by striking out at the person toward whom I am angry. If for some reason I am not able to do that — perhaps for fear of retaliation — then I may act my anger out on some other party, innocent of any current offense.

However, when I act my anger out it is really as if I were trying to drive it away rather than to cherish it. I am doing what I can to shorten the length of its visit with me, in effect. By striking back at the other, I am attempting to eliminate, as it were, the *grounds* for my anger. Once I have attained vengeance, I will no longer feel angry — or so, at least, I think, when I strike back.

A similar situation occurs with fear. Fear sets up what is called the "flight or fight" response. That is, when I am frightened, I am cued to protect myself against whatever is frightening me, to protect myself either by running away or by standing my ground and trying to defend myself. Whichever I select, if I succeed at it I will cease to be afraid, since I will either have removed myself from my threatened position or repelled whatever threatens me. In that way, fear cues me to act in either of two ways, both of which are designed to bring my fear to an end.

Viewed from the perspective opened up by such reflections, fear can be said to be an emotion that tends toward *self-sublation:* an emotion that invites a reaction aimed at *eliminating* the emotion itself as rapidly as possible. As Aristotle also observed of anger, fear is a distressing emotion. It is not — at least not ordinarily — experienced as pleasant; it is experienced as unpleasant or uncomfortable. I don't *like* feeling afraid. Accordingly, when I do feel afraid, I tend to react by trying to get rid of the fear as soon as possible. That is what running away or fighting back promises to accomplish.

Anger is also a self-sublating emotion. In effect, anger cries out to be eliminated immediately. Like hunger or thirst, as well as fear, anger importunately directs me to take action to alleviate it. My hunger tells me to eat; when I do, my hunger ceases. My thirst tells me to drink, so I will no longer be thirsty. My fear tells me to flee or fight, so I will no longer be afraid. My anger tells me to strike back, so I will no longer be angry.

Thus, my anger itself invites me to attempt to drive it away as quickly as possible by striking back or fleeing. By reacting in that way, however, I am actually adopting a stance *against* my anger rather than "cherishing" it, as Thich Nhat Hanh recommends.

"I hate you! I wish you were dead!" Parents know not to take children at their word when they say such things in moments of anger. What loving parents hear in those words is not that their children actually do hate them and want them dead. They know very well that their children really want no such thing. Instead, by saying such things their children are actually telling their parents something very different from what their words, taken in isolation, seem to say. The children are telling their parents something important about what they, the children, are currently feeling, and how much they need their parents' understanding, recognition, and acceptance of those feelings. The children need to be reassured that their parents will continue to be there for them and will continue to nurture them, even when — especially when — the children themselves deliver curses against those very parents. Children need to have their negative feelings toward parents and parental authority — and, more importantly, they need to

SELF-SUBLATING EMOTIONS

Many emotions — including all of the so-called negative emotions such as fear and anger — are "self-sublating." That is, they are emotions which call up reactions designed to make the emotions themselves vanish as quickly as possible. Fear tells me to run away or to fight, for example. If I succeed in doing either, the fear leaves me. In the same way, anger tells me to retaliate against whomever or whatever has angered me; and success at retaliation diminishes my anger. In effect, self-sublating emotions try to get me to drive them away as soon as I can. To accept such self-sublating emotions, listen to them, and learn from them, I must recondition myself *not* to react in the ways those emotions themselves tell me to react.

have *themselves, with* all those disturbing feelings — affirmed by the same parents toward whom those feelings are directed.

For most parents, the automatic reaction to such angry outbursts by their children may well involve some feeling of hurt. Because they feel hurt, parents, in turn, may grow defensively angry themselves — angry at their children for being angry at them. However, it is to be hoped that parents soon learn that such a reaction only makes matters worse. What is needed, instead, is for the parents to stop *reacting* to what their children say in such outbursts of anger and to start *listening* to them, listening to the underlying message conveyed by the outburst. The parents need to listen to what the outburst says about how the children themselves are feeling and, therefore, how they, the parents, can best nurture their children at that time.

If I am going to cherish my own anger, I have to treat it the same way. I have to stop reacting to the anger I feel and instead *listen* to it. Just as children's anger toward their parents can give those parents important information about the children's current needs, so can my own anger give me important information about myself and my own current needs. My anger can give me such information if I will just learn to listen attentively to it rather than trying to drive it away as quickly as possible by acting it out.

I must learn patience with my own anger. I must, if I am ever to be free of anger itself. To free myself of anger I must treat anger, when it comes, with the same patient concern that wise parents show beloved children when the children say they wish their parents dead. Treated with loving patience, children are allowed eventually to outgrow such wishes, along with the frustration and confusion that underlie them. On the other hand, if they are taught that feelings of anger and even rage toward their parents are unacceptable, something not permitted, something only "bad" children would feel, and that such emotions are never to be voiced or otherwise shown, children are denied the opportunity for such growth.

Parents, then, should not react in anger when their children say they wish them dead. However, neither should parents try to grant their children's expressed wish by killing themselves. No more should I necessarily do what my own anger invites me to do: act the anger out by striking back. For parents to commit suicide would hardly be helpful in teaching their children how to deal with such disturbing emotions as frustration, anger, and impatience. It is just as useless for me to try to teach myself how to deal with my own anger by obeying anger's orders to strike back.

By acknowledging and accepting the tumultuous negative feelings of their children, parents help those children learn to acknowledge and accept those same feelings in themselves. And the more children can learn to accept their own negative emotions, the more those children come to understand themselves and their own emotions — and, paradoxically, the *less* tumultuous the children's own emotions become.

The same lesson applies to trying to parent myself. It is neither by refusing to acknowledge such disturbing emotions as anger in myself, nor by directly combating them upon acknowledgment (acknowledging but then actively resisting my anger, for example), nor, certainly, by giving in to them and acting them out, that I give myself a chance eventually to outgrow such emotions. What can transform "negative" or distressing emotions into "positive" ones is neither repression, suppression, nor appeasement. What can transform them is acknowledgment, acceptance, and understanding.

As with any impulse, the angry impulse to strike out or flee rises and falls in reaction to what's going on at the moment. If just given due time, the moment always passes, however. The impulses of the moment will vanish with that moment itself, or soon after, if I just let them. If I do not interfere — interfere by denying, resisting, or acting out my feelings — impulsive emotional reactions such as anger pass away quickly.

It is like being a former smoker, as I am, who still feels impulses to smoke from time to time. Triggered by who knows what old associations in my memory, the impulsive desire to light up a cigarette will occasionally still strike me, even though I quit smoking years ago. Giving in to such impulses by resuming smoking (by deciding to try "just one cigarette," for instance, "just to see what it's like after all this time") would probably be the worst thing I could do under such circumstances. However, refusing to acknowledge temptation — attempting flatly to deny to myself that I sometimes feel such impulses — would be only slightly better, since it could easily lead me to a dangerous underestimation of the power of such impulses when they do strike. Denying the reality of temptation leaves me all the more vulnerable to it.

Finally, resisting such impulses by attempting to drive them away, trying to divert attention to something else or in some other way "getting my mind off it" might work well enough for a while, or when the temptation is slight. It might even work for a time with strong temptations. But my resistance can all too easily be overcome if the temptation grows strong enough, or if I let my guard down. And the latter, letting my guard down, inevitably becomes more likely, the more *successful* I am at warding off repeated attacks of the impulse to smoke.

Thus, such resistance tends, by its very success in the early stages of quitting smoking, to set the smoker up for eventual relapse. The further such a smoker gets from the last smoke, the closer does the smoker get to the next one (to paraphrase a line originally applied to alcoholics struggling to resist the impulse to drink).

In my own case, rather than continuing to rely on any of those three strategies (yielding to the impulse to smoke, denying it, or resisting it by sheer will power), to succeed in quitting smoking I eventually had to learn to apply a simple but difficult lesson: when there's nothing you can do, the best thing to do is nothing. That is, I had to learn neither to act out, deny, or suppress my occasional impulses to smoke, but merely to — let them be. I had to learn the lesson of Little Bo-Peep, whose sheep will surely come home, if only she'll leave them alone.

If I simply observe them rather than acting them out, repressing them, suppressing them, or in some other way interfering with them, my impulses to smoke typically pass away quickly. The impulse to smoke rarely lasts more than a few seconds, at most, if I simply allow it to run its course, neither trying to impede it nor trying to speed it up.

When I first quit smoking, the problem for me as newly abstinent was not really that my impulses to smoke were so strong (strong as they were). Nor was it that any one of those impulses ever lasted so long. Rather, the problem was that there was such a brief interval *between* them.

I had a very heavy cigarette habit (three or more packs a day), and when I first quit smoking, impulses to smoke bombarded me so often that the intervals between them seemed to collapse altogether. Those intervals were still there, I'm sure; but it didn't seem like it at the time.

However, the longer I went without a cigarette, the greater the interval between the impulses to smoke became. Eventually, they came only rarely, at widely varying intervals (though even now they can still gang up on me occasionally, depending on circumstances).

THE PHASES OF AN IMPULSE

Impulsive emotions such as anger or fear follow the same pattern as do all other impulses. All impulses go through a basic five-phase sequence. The first phase is that of the beginning of the impulse, the phase when the impulse is first experienced, when it first rises above the limits of our awareness and begins actually to be felt. In this first phase, the impulse is still relatively weak in intensity, just beginning to build. Next, the impulse goes through a phase of rising intensity, growing in strength until it reaches its peak. That peak is the third phase of the impulse, after which the fourth phase immediately commences, as the impulse now diminishes in intensity, lessens in strength. Finally, in the fifth and final phase, the impulse loses so much strength that it vanishes from experience, sinking once more back beneath the limits of our awareness. Every impulse, including the impulses that characterize such emotions as anger and fear, inevitably goes through those five phases, in order: (1) onset, (2) increase, (3) peak, (4) decrease, and (5) cessation. No matter how strong an impulse may be, or how often it may strike, it will eventually vanish at the fifth and final phase of its process. We just need to be patient and wait it out.

What accounted for the increase of the interval between my impulses to smoke as a function of the length of my abstinence from cigarettes was not anything I really did. It was what I didn't do. For one thing, of course, I didn't give in to those impulses when they did strike: I didn't smoke. But for another, I didn't interfere with them, trying to control their intensity or duration, either. Instead, I just let

THE LESSON OF LITTLE BO-PEEP

In the old nursery rhyme, Little Bo-Peep, who has lost her sheep, is assured that if she will just leave them alone, they are sure to come home. Even if that principle doesn't always work with sheep, it certainly does when it comes to our impulses, which have, in effect, escaped their subliminal pen whenever they become strong enough to bother us. If we will just leave them alone, they will eventually return home. That is, if we just leave our impulses free to pulse, they will eventually pulse themselves out and fall back beneath our awareness, returning to the subliminal pen from which they escaped in the first place.

time, and with it my smoking impulses, pass. And the more time I let pass, the more time passed — namely, between the impulses to smoke.

By letting the impulses to smoke, which inevitably strike ex-smokers even after long abstinence, just run their course, those who successfully quit smoking let those impulses play themselves out, like children who play themselves into exhaustion. As the noise of healthy children's play eventually gives way to the stillness of their sleep, so does the clamor of the impulse to smoke eventually give way to the calm of neutrality toward smoking.

In the same way, if only given sufficient opportunity, the clamor of anger eventually gives way to the calm of forbearance, forgiveness, and resolute decision. To cherish children is to allow them to be children. To cherish anger is to allow anger to be anger — and simply to run its course.

I will fall upon them like a bear robbed of her cubs, and I will tear open the covering of their heart; there I will devour them like a lion, as a wild animal would mangle them.   – HOSEA 13:8

The course of anger, like the course of the impulsive desire to smoke, is to begin, build, peak, diminish, then vanish. To be free of anger is to be free of the need to control anger — control whether, when, and how rapidly it goes through the stages of its course. Although at first glance acting out anger by striking back looks like a natural phase of anger itself, it is actually an endeavor to control anger, to make it go away right now rather than to let it take its own time in leaving. It may be natural (or at least it may have become "second nature") *to me* to act out my anger, but it is not necessarily natural (or even "second-natural") *to anger* to be acted out.

What is natural to anger, as to all feelings, is *to be felt*. Feelings are "for" feeling. For me to cherish anger or any other emotion is simply for me to allow myself to feel the anger as fully as it is there to be felt. I need to allow myself to feel the full weight of my anger, without trying to take anything away from it or add anything to it. Without trying to make it stay or drive it away, I need just to feel it.

Cherishing my anger in that simple, straightforward way — by doing no more than *feeling* it — opens anger to the power of healing and transformation. Very slowly, cherished anger ceases to be angry and instead becomes patient, caring, and resolute.

For centuries Buddhists such as Thich Nhat Hanh have taught that anger can be transformed into *compassion*. Christian monks and mystics throughout many of the same centuries have taught the same lesson in different words: the transformation of anger into love or *charity*. Similar ideas can also be found in other great religious traditions.

Cherished, anger eventually becomes compassion, love, and decisive action. Properly cherished, the red flame of anger becomes the white one of love — a flame that burns without consuming. The heat, the fire of love, its burning passion, comes from transformed anger. Without such nourishment, love can easily grow cold.

Anger, transformed, provides the energy of love, which gives love the fierceness without which it so easily becomes mere sentimentality. Love's fierceness is that of a startled she-bear protecting her cubs, to borrow an image from the Hebrew prophet Hosea. Transformed anger provides the energy love needs to grow powerful, the resources without which love quickly withers, like a seed sown on shallow soil.

Be angry, but don't sin. Don't let the sun go down on your anger.
— Ephesians 4:26

Genuine compassion and charity lie the other side of anger, not this side of it. As noted more than once in Christian Scriptures, doing good for family, friends, or, in general, those with whom I stand connected or toward whom I feel naturally drawn takes no special merit. Everyone does as much. What takes something extra is giving to those not among my own family, friends, and acquaintances, those whom I may actually dislike, and even those who wrong me.

If I forgive only those who do me no wrong, I forgive no one. I have to forgive those who have actually harmed me, or whom I at least perceive to have done so — those the mere thought of whom is often enough to make me angry.

To forgive someone for hurting me is not to deny that I have been hurt. Instead, it is to offer up that very hurt as evidence that I and the one who has hurt me are intimately connected.

When others hurt me I often try to hide the very fact of being hurt from them: I don't want to "give them the satisfaction" of seeing they have hurt me. That is, I want to deny their power *to* hurt me. But to deny others the power to hurt me is to deny that there is any real possibility of connection between us. It is to deny that they can ever really "matter" at all to me. Is it any wonder, then, that such behavior often seems to enrage my persecutors even further, inciting them to hurt me ever more deeply, until finally I do cry out, giving them the "satisfaction" I have tried to deny them — the satisfaction, in the last analysis, of getting me to admit that they really do matter to me, and that, whether I like it or not, they really do have the power to hurt me?

THE EMOTIONS: LETTING THINGS MATTER

If nothing mattered to us, we wouldn't have any emotions. In effect, emotions are the price we pay for letting things matter to us. But think of the alternative! To be without emotions would be to be stones or islands, perhaps, but not human beings — not creatures to whom things matter. Emotions disclose to us ourselves, others, and things, insofar as they *matter* to us. We have emotions, because things do matter to us: their "mattering" to us is what we feel in our "feelings."

To grow beyond anger, it is especially helpful to consider carefully the genuine connections between anger, on the one hand, and forgiveness, on the other. I will use the example of battered women to clarify the main connections between the two.

Too often, the idea that abused women eventually need to "forgive" their abusers is misunderstood. To recommend that a battered woman forgive her abuser is too often taken to mean she should act as if the abuse never occurred in the first place — to act, that is, *as if there were really nothing to be forgiven.* However, the woman who, after repeated abuse, continues to stay with her abusive husband, refuses to file charges against him with the police, and makes no other efforts to protect herself — the woman, that is, who does act as though the abuse never happened in the first place — is not demonstrating *forgiveness.* She is demonstrating fear, confusion, isolation, deprivation, and other signs resulting from, or at least compounded by, the abuse itself.

The idea of "forgiving and forgetting" may make good sense, but it certainly makes no sense to reverse the order and recommend one to "forget and forgive." If I forget before I forgive, there remains nothing to be forgiven, so I could never succeed in carrying out such an order.

In most cases, I cannot just forgive at will. Forgiving becomes less subject to my direct control, the more there is to be forgiven — the more deeply, that is, I am hurt. If someone cuts me off in traffic, I may be able simply to choose to forgive the offense and let it pass from my mind. But I find it much harder to let the cutting remark of one of my colleagues go, let alone being cut out of the life of a close friend. When I most need to forgive — need to, not so much for the sake of the one being forgiven, as for my own sake, so I can get on with my life — is when I find myself least able to do so at will.

The more important it is to forgive, the more forgiveness itself comes only as the culmination of a long process, one that is often painful and difficult. It would be acceptable to counsel battered women or other victims of abuse to forgive their abusers only if such advice came at the *end* of a long journey, one for the making of which victims of abuse would deserve all the help they could get. They would need to be helped to embark on that journey, and then need to be accompanied and supported along the way — not just informed of the ultimate destination and then abandoned with no inkling of how to get there.

Anger is better. There is a sense of being in anger. A reality and presence. An awareness of worth. – Toni Morrison, *The Bluest Eye*

The journey to forgiveness goes *through* anger, not *around* it. Furthermore, just as it does not leave love unaffected, the passage through anger does not leave forgiveness unaffected. Instead, anger gives its strength and energy to forgiveness. That strength and energy reemerge transformed in forgiveness itself, transformed into burning indignation at injustice — and into a pure cry of hurt and pain, unsullied any longer by any defensiveness, desire for vengeance, or other expression of ego-centrism.

Even though any forgiveness (or charity or compassion) worthy of the name must grow on the far side of anger, that is not the same as the far side of hurt or of indignation. To be sure, forgiveness cannot occur where anger is still felt, resentment still nurtured, or ill will still harbored. But forgiveness can develop and thrive in the midst of hurt and indignation — in a world of woe the injustice of which is passionately rejected. In fact, it is only in such a world that forgiveness fully flowers.

The section that follows is a long entry from my personal journal. I wrote it a few years ago, while I was briefly visiting a monastery not far from where I live. It was written at one of the times when I was having to struggle with issues of anger and forgiveness in my own life. The entry tells part of the story of my own effort to journey beyond anger. In this case, my heart is still striving to catch up with my thoughts.

Monday, January 27, 1992

At a discussion with other recovering alcoholics last week, the topic of forgiveness came up, and some of those present were going on about how "confrontation" with others over their behavior is never legitimate. That, coupled with my own recent experiences that involved at least one "confrontation" with [another person] got me thinking.

In fact, what I'm thinking is that: (1) forgiveness (and this is nothing new) clears the ground for genuine reconciliation (as opposed to more subconscious, manipulative blaming/whining/striking-back behavior, which is what will occur if one tries to go "make amends" before one has actually forgiven the other). But (2), even more importantly, forgiveness itself can only come once the wound has been allowed to close. That is, one must first own up to one's own anger and hurt — letting oneself feel them and accept them, then sorting out what is legitimate from what is not legitimate in them (e.g., getting inappropriate, neurotic emotion out of the way) — before one can become willing to let them go. But only someone who can let the anger go can forgive the person at whom the anger is directed: to hold on to anger toward the other is precisely to resent the other; it is to *refuse* to forgive.

Thus, the key to forgiveness lies in *learning how properly to love oneself, to care for oneself.* We can't force ourselves to forgive any more than we can force ourselves to love, or to feel any other feeling. But the ordinary wisdom is that the road to genuine forgiveness is to act as if one had already forgiven: e.g., pray for the other person, even when you hate that person. In contrast, it seems to me that we need to face our own anger and heal it through acceptance and love if we are ever to become forgiving toward others. And doing that will often require that we confront the others about their behavior by sharing our own anger and hurt with them.

It is such very confrontation that allows the wound to heal, so that forgiveness can then be offered.

When AA's "Big Book," on the ninth step of AA's Twelve Steps — the ninth step suggesting that alcoholics in recovery make amends to anyone we have harmed by our past behavior — says that we alcoholics in recovery must confine our attention to discussing with those to whom we are making amends what *we* have done wrong, never bringing up what the *other* has done, but dealing solely with *our* fault in the affair, it is not going against what I'm saying, I think.

First, what the Big Book says is said in the context of *wrongs* we have done others. But if we properly confront others about their anger-provoking behavior *at the time it occurs*, then no wrong accrues to us. The wrong is to build or hold a *resentment*. If I learn how to confront others — which is to say, learn to "own" my own feelings of anger and act appropriately on them — then I don't let any resentment build to begin with.

If a resentment *has* built, then my wrong is *not to have been honest with the others in the first place* (as I would have been in confronting them properly). Accordingly, my "amend" would consist of (1) going to them, if appropriate, and asking their forgiveness for having been *dishonest* with them in the past and, thus, allowing resentment toward them to develop in me; and then (2) committing myself to being honest with them in the future.

Forgiveness is an expression of *strength*, not of *weakness*; it is *resentment* that comes from weakness — cf. Nietzsche and Scheler (two German philosophers who wrote about resentment). When I am sound and whole, then I am able to forgive. But when I am weak and hurt, then I must first find *healing* (whole-ing) before I can forgive. I must *convalesce* first.

But that makes forgiveness, in the full sense, a relationship between equals. Or, better, it *establishes* equality. To the extent that I am able to remain spiritually sound and healthy even when the blows of others rain down on me, only to that extent can I forgive them; and in forgiving them I rise above the subordinated state into which I have been hurled (or let myself be hurled) by their actions and lay claim again to my integrity (which etymologically means my untouchableness: inviolability and inviolateness), despite and beyond their grasp upon me.

Hence, to imitate Christ, for example, by practicing the perfect forgiveness attributed to him would require nurturing oneself into as much wholeness-healthiness as possible, making maximal forgiveness toward others possible.

All too often we go at it in exactly the wrong way: since Christ forgave his persecutors, I should forgive mine. However, since I *cannot*, despite how hard I try — since the resentment itself still smolders, no matter how hard I try to deny it — I turn my anger *inward* as well as outward. I condemn myself for my own failure to forgive — to forgive more than I am able *to* forgive. But that actually *decreases* my capacity for forgiveness and *increases* my sensitivity to injury, since the need to preserve my ever-lessening sense of self-worth feeds that sensitivity. Paradoxically, then, this misunderstood attempt to imitate Christ makes me less, rather than more, Christlike.

But when we are in a situation of *in*equality, how can we practice forgiveness, if, as I have been writing, forgiveness is an establishing of equality?

Again, the way we tend to go at it is all wrong, I think. We try to "rise above it all" — try, in effect, to *deny* our hurt: "I won't let them get to me."

But if the model is Christ, then that is not at all what *he* did. When persecuted, he was not at all "above" it all. He *suffered.* He wept, bled, hurt, thirsted, hungered, felt desolate and forsaken. He died and was buried, in fact.

By that model what we should do, when those who have power over us (as the Romans had over the man Jesus) persecute us, is not to deny our pain, but to *affirm* it: to allow ourselves the fullest *expression* of our suffering, just as Christ did. In that sense, there was nothing "stoical" about him. The "stoicism" (which is not really the right word any longer) — the "abandonment," the "resignation" — was at an altogether different level: not a resignation that somehow *lessens* the pain (a *c'est la vie* sort of approach), but one that grants the pain full scope, accepting and affirming it, abandoning oneself, in trust, to it.

The capacity to forgive even those who torment us unjustly lies not in pretending that we are not tormented or pretending that they really "cannot hurt us." It lies, rather, in *abandoning ourselves to* the torment they inflict. Not a "stiff-upper-lip," "won't-give-them-the-satisfaction-of-seeing-how-much-they-hurt-me" approach, but rather releasing ourselves to the full expression of how deeply they *have* hurt us — a crying out as does the child when hurt or frightened or betrayed.

In the cry of the child the child asserts equality. In the assertion "You have hurt me" lies acknowledgment of the other and of the capacity of the other to hurt me — acknowledgment of our genuine *community* with one another.

And in the depths of that cry of suffering lies the strength of forgiveness. Not: "I forgive you because what you did didn't really hurt me all that much." Rather: "I forgive you for the deep hurt you have inflicted on me because I *accept* that hurt, I affirm myself *as* deeply wounded, and find strength in that self-affirming acceptance to let my anger and rage and desire for vengeance go. I don't need to avenge myself because I am fully occupied in just letting myself be hurt by your actions. I don't hold it against you, because in my agony all I can do is reach *out* to you, my cry of pain itself forgiving you at the very time it protests against my suffering by bearing witness to it and calling out for you to embrace and comfort me in my need.

One loves one's enemies by openly acknowledging how deeply their enmity hurts one.

Self-Evaluation

How angry are you? Before you can begin to grow beyond anger, you must first grow into it, in effect. That is, you must accept the anger in yourself. For most of us, that is difficult to do. In our culture especially, it is difficult for many people to acknowledge their own anger even to themselves, let alone to others. It is especially important for such people to learn accurately to assess the nature, focus, and intensity of their own anger. They need to take an "anger inventory."

- To begin your own anger inventory, ask yourself how you feel about anger itself. For example, you may be one of the many in our society today whose basic emotional response to anger is negative. If so, then you may feel guilty or ashamed whenever you grow angry at someone, especially if you do or say anything to express that anger. If that negative way is how you tend to respond emotionally to anger, then in order to arrive at an honest, accurate assessment of how much anger you actually feel in your own life, you will have to suspend or bracket such negative responses. If you don't, they will distort your assessment.

- After having done that preliminary work, go on to your actual anger inventory. Look especially for any patterns that may emerge. In doing so, be sure to include asking yourself how much of your anger is the anger of indignation, and how much is the anger of defense. After all, the ultimate purpose of your "anger inventory" is the same as that of any inventory: to determine what you should keep "in stock" and what you should throw out.

Disciplines, Practices, Exercises

First of all, continue any and all of the practices you find useful and informative from the end of chapter 2, especially keeping an "anger log." If you did not already take that suggestion from chapter 2, now would be a good time to reconsider it. In addition, here is a new tool you can add to your toolbox for working on your emotional literacy. It can be used in connection with the discipline of keeping a daily anger log, or it can stand as a complete discipline of its own. I have borrowed it from AA's Big Book, with modifications for general use.

- When you find yourself growing angry, instead of either acting the anger out or repressing it, try analyzing it. To do so, use paper and pen or pencil. Make four columns on your paper.

  Label the first column "Who/What I'm Angry At." Then write the name of the person or thing (for example, your car, or the IRS) toward whom you feel anger. Label the next column "Why." Here, write whatever it was that occasioned your anger: what the person did or said (or didn't do, or represents) that "made" you angry. Next, label the third column "Affecting My...." Then write how it was that what you've just listed as the cause of your anger affected you, such that it brought your anger on in the first place. AA's Big Book suggests that our responses in this column will always or almost always fall under one, two, or more — often, all — of four basic categories. Either the event that sets me off affects: (1) my self-esteem; (2) my security — financial or, I would add, emotional; (3) my ambitions, including not only grandiose plans but also the simplest wants and desires; or (4) my personal relationships. Finally, in the fourth column trace what I call your own "anger fault-lines," the lines running through your personal character connecting the points at which "slippage" into anger is most liable to occur in your life. To fill out this fourth column, ask yourself just what "stress point" there is in you, such that the particular person or object in question, doing or being the particular thing at issue, caused anger as your reaction. What is it in you that opened you to the possibility of anger in the first place? For example, it may be pride, envy, "people pleasing," or some other "character defect," or because you placed unreasonable expectations on yourself or others.

The point of the fourth column — and, therewith, of the whole exercise — is to identify those aspects of your own character or habitual patterns of behavior that make you particularly susceptible to anger. Then, once you've identified those "stress points," you may be able to do something about them, something effective for helping yourself to grow beyond anger. The general principle is that by lessening your *irritability* you are bound to lessen the actual *irritations* you will experience in your life.

– Four –

Afraid to Fear

We have nothing to fear but fear itself.
– Franklin D. Roosevelt

President Roosevelt delivered that famous line during the worst days of the Great Depression. Europe was in turmoil, Japanese military aggression was already beginning in Asia, and World War II was only a few years away. The president's words were meant to offer encouragement and hope. However, they have never sounded especially encouraging to me.

For most of my life, fear itself seemed more than enough to have to fear. I lived for years in a state of constant underlying fear of fear itself. I was so afraid of fear, in fact, that I lived in complete subjection to it.

Like anger, fear is a distressing emotion. It is painful. I didn't like feeling afraid. So I tried to flee fear, to run away from it. I tried to protect myself against feeling fear.

Unfortunately, since my efforts to protect myself were themselves motivated by fear (namely, my fear of fear itself), the more successful I was at protecting myself against fear, the more threatened by it I felt. That is, the more afraid I grew. The more I managed to isolate myself from fear, the more need I felt to isolate myself further.

By the end of my drinking career I had isolated myself so completely that I didn't know a single one of my neighbors by name, even though we had been living in the same house for six years by that time. By then there was only one person among my acquaintances I considered a friend, a man with whom I did much of my drinking. I spent all of my time either at work, in a bar, or at home. Whenever

I had to venture beyond those three well-known "safe" places, fear would be waiting for me. So I tried never to venture beyond them.

But even that was not enough. Even if I didn't go out where it could catch me, fear could still come banging on my door — or, more likely, ringing my doorbell. Accordingly, if I was alone at home and the doorbell rang, I simply didn't answer it. If my wife or son was around when it rang, I made them answer it. I would retreat to the bathroom and hide there until whoever it was at the door had gone away. Sometimes, I had to stay in the bathroom a long time.

In addition to ringing the doorbell, fear might also ring the phone. So I didn't answer that either. Whoever else might be home to answer it had standing instructions that I was "not there" if the call happened to be for me. Towards the end, it rarely was.

Since I was afraid of fear, I carefully avoided letting myself know the real reason I did such things — that it was actually the very fear I was so afraid of that was motivating my behavior. Instead, I always had some good excuse for not answering the phone or the door and for spending so much time in the bathroom. In that way, like a trustee at my own jail, I helped fear hold me captive.

It was only once I finally began to learn how to feel that I gradually discovered fear itself was really not so frightening. I slowly came to understand that fear itself was not really such a threat. I learned that fear alone wouldn't kill me.

On the other hand, I also came to see that the fear of fear might. In fact, during all the years before I began to learn how to feel, the fear of my own fear had been trying to choke me to death. By the end, it had almost succeeded. By then, for all intents and purposes I was already dead. It was just that my body hadn't heard the news yet, so it was still walking around.

Ironically, it turned out to be the very fear I was so afraid of that eventually managed to breathe some life back into me. Somehow, driving home after my last drunk, I let my guard down for a moment, and fear struck. The veil of illusion and self-deception with which I'd so long surrounded myself fell for a moment, and I saw myself clearly, finally reflected in a nondistorting mirror.

THE FLIGHT FROM FEAR

Aristotle says that fear, like anger, is a "distressed" state. That is, we experience the state as itself distressing or upsetting. Fear doesn't feel "good" to us. Rather, it feels unpleasant. It "agitates" us, we could say. Accordingly, we tend to flee not only from what frightens us, but also from the feeling of fear itself. We deny our own fear. We try to hide it from ourselves, like the proverbial "boy whistling in the dark." As an emotion, fear itself brings with it this dimension of covering itself over — of casting us into a headlong rush to escape: a flight from fear. In that sense, the fear of fear itself is built into all fear, regardless of what else may be the focus of the fear.

I didn't like what I saw. What was especially appalling was to see that the thing in the mirror was myself. That meant there was no longer any possibility of escape.

At that moment, I was left with only one option. I had to start learning how to feel.

Remarkably, the more I learned how to feel, the less what I felt was fear. It turned out that my emotional illiteracy and my fear were reciprocally implicated in one another: each reinforced the other.

Fear comes from ignorance. At least the fear I spent so much of my life being afraid of does.

In *Being and Time* the twentieth-century philosopher Martin Heidegger says that fear is an emotion to which one remains open only to the extent that one is not oneself. In effect, according to him, I am subject to attacks of fear only insofar as I remain wrapped in ignorance about who I truly am. The note of fear will sound in me only if I am out of tune with myself.

Since I began to overcome my emotional illiteracy I have often pondered Heidegger's remarks about fear. From an unexpected source, I gained new insight into those remarks, the light they cast on fear itself and, above all, on my own fear of it. That new insight came to me from reading something by a very different sort of author, one who was not from the twentieth century, but from the sixth. Nor was he a highly learned professor. Instead — at least according to Pope Gregory the Great, his first biographer — he was "wisely uneducated." He was, in fact, nothing more than a simple monk. But he was to enter history as a saint, and as the source of what became (and still remains) the main form of Western Christian monasticism: St. Benedict of Nursia, the otherwise all but anonymous author of a short and simple Rule by which life in Benedictine monasteries is still governed.

The course of my own emotional education, begun only in my forties, eventually led me to St. Benedict's Rule and to the still vital monastic tradition based upon it. It led me into visiting more than one Benedictine monastery. In time it even led me to become a Benedictine "oblate" myself.

A modern Benedictine oblate is a layperson who feels so strongly attracted to Benedictine spirituality that he or she chooses to become formally affiliated with some one specific Benedictine monastery, but without actually becoming a monk. Oblates are part of the "extended family" of the monastic community, as it were.

Most modern oblates continue to live in their own private homes rather than moving into the monastery, as those becoming monks would. They do not leave their spouses, children, and other relatives, nor do they usually abandon their jobs or professions. They just try to support their monastery as they are able, visiting when they can, and to live their own ongoing lives in accordance with the spirit of Benedictine monasticism and of St. Benedict's Rule, which they are encouraged to read and reread, to ponder and apply to their own lives, just as monks try to do.

As an oblate, that is what I try to do. In the process, I have learned many lessons that have been valuable for my emotional education, including one on fear.

The first step of humility, then, is that one keeps the fear of God always before one's eyes and never forgets it.

— *The Rule of St. Benedict*

In the seventh chapter of his Rule St. Benedict discusses humility. In that context he also makes some remarks about fear. Benedict imagines humility to be like a ladder the monk has to climb. The ladder has twelve rungs. The first and lowest rung, he says, is to keep "the fear of God" always before the mind's eye. From the first time I read the Rule, that idea gave me pause, especially given my Heideggerian background. According to Benedict, for a monk it is only by arduously climbing the ladder of humility that one can truly become who one is. But if, as Heidegger maintains, I am subject to fear only when I am *not* myself, only when I am living in ignorance of who I truly am, how could Benedict be right to claim that the road of humility, which is supposed to lead one to one's true self, starts with the fear of God? Unless Benedict's "fear of God" is altogether different from the "fear" Heidegger has in mind, the saint and the philosopher would contradict one another.

Through my ongoing emotional education, I have come to experience that the two "fears" are indeed very different. But they are also concretely interconnected. They are so different, yet interconnected, in fact, that the sort of fear Heidegger addresses is possible only on the basis of a headlong rush — a frightened fleeing — *from* the fear of the sort Benedict calls the fear of God. In effect, being afraid of what Benedict calls the fear of God is what delivers me over to every other fear, in which I lose myself. In that sense, the root of all other fears — fear of spiders, of snakes, or of appearing naked in public, for example — could be said to be the fear of *that* singular fear: the root of all other fears would consist of being afraid to fear God.

What fear fears for, is precisely the one who is afraid.
— MARTIN HEIDEGGER, *Being and Time*

My ordinary, everyday fears feed upon uncertainty and confusion. The fear in them is what I typically feel when I say that I am "afraid of" something. This is fear in the sense that I might be afraid of the dark or of strangers. It is the fear of snakes, dogs, rats, or spiders, of loud noises or crowded places, of crossing bridges, walking under ladders or riding elevators, of flying or driving, of heights, caves, or open spaces, of "ghoulies and ghosties and long-leggedy beasties and things that go bump in the night."

In the fourth century C.E. St. Hilary of Poitiers gave some other common examples of such fears. His list is interesting. It includes all of the following: the fear that can be brought on by a guilty conscience (fear that I might be found out, and of the consequences of that happening), fear of offending someone more powerful, fear of being attacked by someone stronger, fear of sickness, and fear of encountering some wild beast. In general, Hilary observes, this fear is what is at issue whenever I am afraid of "suffering evil in any form."

In the sense appropriate to Hilary's remark, the "evils" I am afraid of suffering have nothing demonic or diabolical about them. They don't necessarily involve any *moral* evil — any intentional malice or injustice — at all. Instead, they are evils in the sense of "harms," of something that in some way causes me suffering.

Sometimes the suffering might be physical, as when Job was struck with boils. Sometimes it would be emotional, as when a loved one dies. At times my self-esteem is damaged, as when events frustrate my ambitions, whether for financial security, emotional support, public recognition, social approval, or whatever.

What is common to all of these cases, however, is the way they are *centered on myself.* All of the harms involved are harms *to me.* They are harms that befall *my* body, *my* ambitions, *my* reputation, *my* status, *my* bank account.

Sometimes the harm strikes me directly. That is what happens to Job when he is struck with his boils, for example. At other times, I am only indirectly harmed, through direct harm visited upon some other person or thing with which I have come to identify myself. For example, I may suffer because "my" hometown football team loses a game.

As Hilary remarks, these fears are forms of "the trepidation our weak humanity feels when it is afraid of suffering something it does not want to happen." When I experience such fear, it is always *my own* wants, *my* desires, needs, and plans, that are uppermost: fear that something *I* do not want to happen to me will happen despite my not wanting it to happen.

Thus, in all such common, everyday fears — such things as fear of strangers or fear of speaking in public — not only am I the one who is afraid, the one who feels the fear; in all of them I am also the one *for* whom I fear, the person for the sake of whom I am concerned. I am concerned that *I* might undergo harm, and concerned to avoid that happening. In that sense, all such fear remains *I*-centered, *self*-centered — "ego-centric." In one way or another, in everyday fear it is harm to my ego that I fear. Everyday fears are the ego's fears for the ego itself.

Though my own ego would rather not admit it, my own fears, for the most part, have always been self-centered, in the sense just explained. They have tended to be ultimately egocentric even when, on the surface, my fears appear to demonstrate concern for the welfare of others. For example, when one of my children has come home from school with a less than perfect report card, I must admit that at least part of my initial reaction has been for my own sake rather than for my child's. Through my mind have flitted thoughts of comparison between my child and other parents' children, comparisons which might make me jealous: quite for my own sake, I want my child's star to

THE EGO-CENTRISM OF EVERYDAY FEAR

In one way or another, everyday fears are always self-centered, "ego-centric." When I am afraid, it is always for my own sake that I am frightened. Sometimes I am frightened for my own sake directly. In that case I feel threatened in some aspect of my own person or life. Or else I am frightened indirectly for my own sake, through being directly frightened for someone or something I regard as "mine" ("my" wife, "my" children, "my" country) — someone or something or with which I identify myself ("my" hometown football team, perhaps). Everyday fear is fear of what I perceive as threatening to me or mine.

shine more brightly (or at least no less so) than the stars of other children. After all, it is *my* child at issue!

They become audacious with God and lose holy fear, which is the key to and guardian of all the virtues.
     – St. John of the Cross, *Dark Night of the Soul*

As it operates in Benedict's Rule, genuine fear of *God* is an altogether different sort of fear. Indeed, at least so long as I experience it, the fear involved in "fear of God" actually works to liberate me from all my everyday fears. It opens before me the possibility of becoming free of them, by overcoming the underlying "trepidation" that Hilary, Benedict's predecessor, says lies at the root of them all.

What Benedict and many others in the Christian tradition have experienced as the fear of God, those who come from different traditions, or even those with no living tradition from which they draw inspiration and sustenance, can also experience. It is just that for them

the experience does not come packaged, as it were, as the fear *of God*.
I will return to that point shortly. For now, however, I will stay within
the perspective and language of "God."

To continue speaking that language, the fear of God is nothing like
the fears already considered, fears of "suffering evil in any form." To
fear God is not to feel afraid *of* God — in the sense, for example,
of fearing that God might punish me for something I am thinking
of doing (as a child might fear an abusive father who grows irritated
at her for something she has done or failed to do). To fear God in
that way would be to commit a form of *idolatry*. It would be to substitute for the idea of a God who transcends human categories of
thought the idea of some being who differs not in kind but only in
degree from someone who is merely more powerful than I am, someone of whom I am afraid because he might use his power to harm
me if I displease him. To fear God in that way would be to substitute
an image of my own making for God, and then to bow down and
worship that image.

It is only when I cease to be afraid of God in such an idolatrous
way — that is, cease to fear the idol I have substituted for God — that
I begin truly to fear God in Benedict's and Hilary's sense. Or, rather,
it is the fear of God that *dispels* my being afraid of God. It dispels fear
of idols by removing the "trepidation" that lies at its root. The fear of
God teaches me that I really have nothing to fear, so long as I remain
in right relation to God — which I do precisely *by* "fearing God," by
being a "God-fearing person." So long as I fear God (*God*, not some
idol), "what can mere mortals do to me," as the Psalmist asks?

Unlike everyday fear, the fear of trepidation, the reaction to which
is to get set to fight or flee from what I fear, the fear of God does not
cause me to draw away from God or to defend myself against God.
It does not trigger a fight-or-flight response toward God. Instead, it
invites me to draw nearer to God and to let down my defenses toward
God. That is why Hilary, for example, can identify the fear of God
with the *love* of God, saying that to fear God *is* to love God. The fear
of God invites me to draw close to God and to enter into intimacy —
into union — with God.

❖

So to be drawn into union with God is to be "ravished" by God, to use the poet John Donne's way of putting it. To fear God is to experience God's beauty, experience that God is truly "a ravishing beauty."

As some common expressions reveal, sometimes we are struck by a beauty so great that it makes us *ache*, that it *wracks* us. Experiencing such beauty is so exquisitely painful that we feel as though we will die of it. It seems to be more than we can bear.

Such beauty is not for the timid or faint of heart. To continue to hold oneself open to it requires courage. One can lose oneself in such beauty, and, if one is not careful, one will.

And yet, perhaps only cowards would be careful in such circumstances. Perhaps, like fools, the brave will rush ahead, even if it is to their own death. Indeed, fully to experience the fear of God *is* to die, in an important sense. To enter into the fear of God, to stand in the open before God, letting God be God, in all God's might and majesty, is to die to the "self," the "ego." It is to be emptied of ego and all its vanities.

The fear of God kills the ego, the "I" who worships only idols — its own self-projections. The ego cannot see the face of God and live. To hold myself open to God in fear can be possible to me at all only if I am more than my ego, only if I am more than "I."

When I am struck by the fear of God, it feels like I will die. I feel that I cannot bear it. Not surprisingly, therefore, my natural response is to resist that feeling of fear, to deny it. I attempt to flee from that fear. I fling myself away from it.

Flinging myself away *from* that singular fear means flinging myself away from God, who is revealed *as* God only *in* such fear. Flinging myself from God, I fling myself *into* everyday "fearfulness." I would much rather fear idols, which are finally no more than projections of myself, than fear God, who wildly exceeds all my projections. Afraid of the fear of God because it feels to me like my own death (which is precisely what it is, for the only "I" I know, at least this side of the fear of God), I would rather fear anything else. I would rather feel fear toward *everything* else, just so long as I do not have to fear *that* particular fear. Only if I find myself cornered, with no way out, will I finally let myself fear God.

> *Fear is anxiety . . . hidden from itself.*
> — MARTIN HEIDEGGER, *Being and Time*

Not long after I was born, when my father was still a young man, he had a terrible motorcycle accident. He was a motorcycle enthusiast long before it became fashionable. One evening he and a friend took a ride. At one point they were traveling along a deserted highway west of Denver on a moonless night, doing sixty miles an hour.

My father hit head-on a pile of broken chunks of asphalt, left unmarked in the middle of the road by a paving crew. His bike ended up in a farmer's field, relatively undamaged. My father ended up further ahead down the highway, bouncing face-first along it. Many weeks and much reconstructive surgery later, he walked out of the hospital (soon to resume his seat on his newly repaired motorcycle).

I remember my father, when I was a child, telling with relish the story of how, as his motorcycle was roaring off into the field and my father himself was turning head-over-heels through the cold night air before coming back to earth, an utter, peaceful calm descended upon him. As he spun through the air, he related, he felt no fear, no worry or concern, only stillness and silence. He always remembered remarking to himself, just before his head struck the highway, how beautiful and clear the lights of Denver were that night, gleaming in the distance.

My father was not above exaggeration for the sake of a good story. So, growing up at home I used to take his account of that accident with more than a grain of salt. That was until I had a similar experience of my own (with a car rather than a motorcycle, and with a very different set of circumstances). Then I learned to appreciate the exactness of his description.

Day by day remind yourself that you are going to die.
                                        The Rule of St. Benedict

It is an old theme: the sudden, unexpected appearance on the scene of death in its certainty can bring on a state of uncanny clarity. In the face of death, priorities sort themselves out definitively by rank. Petty concerns fall away; only what really counts remains. The grip of everyday worries and troubles is broken, and the possibility of actually living life to the full, rather than just living through it, comes into view. Decision replaces distraction.

I remember once, in a meeting of alcoholics in recovery, that a young man who had only recently begun attending regularly expressed fear about an upcoming IRS audit. The next member to speak suggested that the previous speaker reflect upon just what the IRS could actually do to him. Even if the worst-case scenario came to pass, so what? "After all," the second speaker ended, "they can't eat you." "Oh, yes, they can!" piped up a third person. "But that doesn't matter."

Encounters with death such as my father's momentarily open the door to a way of living in which death itself is never forgotten. For that very reason, it is also a way of living which is free of worry, distraction, and apprehension about dying. If I could live in the constant remembrance of my own mortality, I could live free of any "trepidation" about death, to use St. Hilary's term. *Knowing* I will die, I would no longer be afraid of death. If I were still afraid of anything pertaining to my own death, it would be that I might slip back into *forgetfulness* of death, becoming lost again in a thicket of petty worries and trepidations, robbing me of the chance to *live* my life.

In such a state, my *fearfulness before* death — my attempts *not* to let myself know anything about it — would vanish like fog in the bright light of the *fear of* death. To fear death, in that sense of the expression, would be to strive to live in the constant awareness of my own mortality, the constant "recollection" of my own death, rather than to fall back into forgetfulness of it. It would be constantly to let death re-collect *me* into my own life in its uniqueness.

There would be nothing morbid about trying to live in such constant awareness of death. Quite the opposite. The fear of death would free me from all morbidity, all morbid fascination with death.

What underlies morbidity is not the fear of death, but being afraid of it. When I am so frightened by something that I must do all I can to avoid it, it exercises a strange fascination over me. When I am so afraid, my fear keeps me glued to what I am so afraid of, like a rabbit paralyzed by the lights of the car about to run it over.

In contrast, what I am calling the fear of death brings me, as Heidegger puts it, freedom *toward* death. It frees me from morbid fascination with death, gets me unstuck before death's gaze. The person who fears death is no longer afraid to die. Rather, if he or she remains afraid at all, it is a matter of being afraid *not to live* — afraid that death may come without that person ever really having lived at all.

If I am not afraid to fear death, I will not waste my time on petty, meaningless concerns. I will not run away from myself and the realities of my life to find distraction in television, drugs, politics, sex, or work. Only someone who has no fear of death, someone who has forgotten death, risks frittering life away in such pursuits.

"Fear of God," "fear of death" — both expressions point in the same direction, that of the *liberation* from the timidity and fearfulness that limit me in so many ways, making me afraid to try new things, go new places, meet new people, or think new thoughts. Both point in the direction of getting free of the fear of fear itself, what President Roosevelt said was all we really had to fear in the first place.

(That is not to say that there is no difference between the two, fear of God and fear of death. There is. The difference, however, lies in the liberty into which they open the way, not in the bondage from which they provide release.)

FEAR OF DEATH, FEAR OF LIVING

The less passionately we embrace life, the more we fear death in an inauthentic way — fear it as something to be avoided. Paradoxically, those who are most afraid of death in this way are those who live the most constricted lives. What manifests itself as such inauthentic fear of death is actually most often an underlying fear of living. It is a fear of living life to the full, of striking out boldly into the unknown in one's choices and actions. At the root of such fearfulness, such hesitation in the face of life and its demands, is a basic sense of personal insecurity.

In contrast, the authentic fear of death releases us from the fear of living. It liberates us to live life fully and passionately. It is this authentic fear of death — which is, in effect, the fear of dying without ever having lived — that spiritual teachers such as St. Benedict recommend we always keep focused in our minds. Such authentic fear of death nourishes the sense of genuine freedom that can come only with a deep sense of personal security.

When alcoholics first hit bottom and begin the struggle to recover from alcoholism, what most motivates them to maintain sobriety is the fear of slipping back into the life of drinking. In fact, the difference between an alcoholic who has really hit bottom and is at last ready to start to learn how to live sober, and one who is still not quite done drinking, is that the former has come to abhor drinking itself, whereas the latter at most wants to avoid the negative consequences of continuing to drink.

For a while — sometimes a long while — after sobering up, the alcoholic who has turned the corner into recovery will often have to fight mightily against the temptation to drink again. It may take all of the alcoholic's strength of will to resist such temptation. During that period, fear of the consequences of drinking again (fear of losing a job or a spouse, of being jailed or ruined financially, and so forth) will probably not provide enough motivation for the alcoholic to continue such resistance. Even if fear of the *consequences* of drinking again does prove adequate to weather the storms of temptation that gather during early sobriety, it is likely not to prove adequate for withstanding the alcoholic's very success resisting such temptation.

What makes the very success at staying sober dangerous for the alcoholic is that, as sobriety continues to protect the alcoholic from the consequences of drinking, the fear of those same consequences grows less acute. Eventually, the alcoholic who refrains from drinking only because of fearing the consequences if he doesn't is likely to lose the sense of any present motive for continuing to refrain. At some point, even the most passing temptation to drink is liable to seem more than enough to justify a return to drinking — until the next time the consequences become severe enough to motivate another spell of "going on the wagon," when the whole useless cycle begins again.

In contrast, the alcoholic who has finally come to abhor drinking as such, and not merely the probable negative consequences of drinking, stands a much better chance — an excellent one, in fact — of maintaining sobriety. What motivates such an alcoholic to stay sober is no longer fear of the consequences of drinking, but fear of lapsing back into drinking itself, even regardless of the consequences. The fear is no longer one of suffering something as a result of drinking; it is the fear of suffering drinking itself again. It is the fear of once more losing my life to the bottle, even if I am able to keep everything else, job, spouse, car, home, reputation, and status included.

The alcoholic who has truly turned the corner into recovery no longer fears punishments *for* drinking. Instead, the alcoholic now fears the punishment *of* drinking. Drinking itself has become, for that alcoholic, its own punishment; and it is fear of *that* punishment that makes the alcoholic willing to go to any lengths to avoid "relapse."

Unlike the alcoholic who merely wants to avoid the negative consequences of drinking, the alcoholic who has come to abhor drinking itself will find that success in maintaining sobriety makes it easier to continue maintaining it. For the drinker motivated by fear of the *consequences* for taking a drink, the very success at staying away from alcohol, as just remarked, lessens the very fear that provides the motive for *continuing* to stay sober. But for the drinker motivated by the fear of drinking itself, regardless of the consequences, staying away from alcohol only *strengthens* the underlying, motivating fear. That is because success at abstaining from alcohol begins to change the fear of drinking that initially motivates abstinence into something new.

As an alcoholic in recovery myself, my own initial motive for not drinking was precisely the second sort of fear, the fear of once again becoming what I was before I hit bottom. For a while after I first stopped drinking, all of my efforts in recovery were animated by my newfound abhorrence of my old self, the person I used to be — and continued to be, right up until, hitting bottom, I finally came to myself and was repelled by what I had become.

However, as I continued in recovery, more and more that old self dropped away. More and more, I became "a different man" than I used to be (like Scrooge in Dickens's *Christmas Carol* becoming, after his night of visitation by the spirits, the best keeper of Christmas there ever was). Progressively, my old motivation of avoiding relapse, avoiding the possibility of drinking again, was replaced by a newfound enthusiasm for sobriety itself, an exuberance for my new life free of alcohol, that life with all its ups and downs, its pains as well as its pleasures. The fear of drinking gave way *as a motive* to the joy of continuing sobriety.

In the same way, the fear of death begins with a moment of shattering awareness, an awareness, namely, that so far I have not really lived at all. My fearfulness has kept me from living. For life in all its richness and diversity, I have substituted mere timid existence (a death-in-life, a living death).

The truth of this lifeless "life" reveals itself to me most clearly and forcefully at the emotional level, in the disgust and repulsion I feel toward myself during such moments of insight. It is that repulsion itself, that self-disgust, that motivates me to reach out for help and open myself to change. At such moments I feel willing to do anything, whatever I must, to avoid lapsing back into that old way of existing, of merely living *through* my life, without ever *living* it.

> ... *all that he once performed with dread, he will now begin to observe without effort, as though naturally, from habit, no longer out of fear of hell, but out of love of Christ, good habit and delight in virtue.* — *The Rule of St. Benedict*

So it is, too, for those who speak the relevant language, with the "fear of God." When I am brought to stand before God and made to experience God as God — that living God into whose hands, according to the author of the Letter to the Hebrews, it is a terrible thing to fall — I am brought, as well, to stand revealed to myself as *I* am *before* God. That is, I am brought face to face with my own insignificance before, and my utter dependence upon, God.

The light in which I see myself during such experience penetrates the darkest corners of my soul. It leaves no more shadows in which any part of me might hide. Whatever may be hideous and repulsive in me, whatever shies away from the light, is brought out into the open, its hideousness now heightened immeasurably by contrast with the purity of the light surrounding it. I stand revealed to myself in all of what St. Benedict and other Christians would call my "sinfulness" — my "fallen" condition — my bondage, despite myself and my own efforts, to what the Apostle Paul calls "the flesh." I experience how I have turned away from God, from the light, and strayed deeper and deeper into the darkness of life lived in the absence of God — strayed into the *forgetfulness* of God — through my failure to keep the *fear* of God always "before my mind," as Benedict recommends.

Accordingly, when struck by the fear of God I recoil from the very thought of this self now revealed to me (myself lost in the forgetfulness of God), just as the alcoholic hitting bottom and turning around

LOVE AND FEAR

Love drives out everyday fear, but fulfills authentic fear.
Everyday fear gives me a motive for avoiding what I fear.
Love, however, draws me toward what I love. Accordingly,
love and everyday fear are incompatible: where the one
enters, the other must exit. In contrast, authentic fear
motivates me to avoid anything that would come between
me and what I fear. It clears the way for me to draw closer.
Thus, such authentic fear comes to completion in love. It
is itself already love, in an initial stage of its development.

toward recovery recoils from the thought of drinking again. Like the
alcoholic, I am willing, at least so long as the memory of what I have
been allowed to see in that moment of shattering vision remains vivid
in my mind, to do whatever I must to escape from my old way of
being and to keep from lapsing back into it again. I am driven forward by the fear of returning to sin, falling back into forgetfulness,
in the same way that the alcoholic in early recovery is driven forward by the fear of returning to drink. Just as the return to drinking
now strikes the alcoholic as its own worst punishment, so does the
return to a life forgetful of God, a life lived with no fear of God,
now strike me as already the worst of all possible punishments. It now
seems to me that to fall back into such forgetfulness would be "hell."
Hence, as Benedict also says, the fear of God begins as the fear of
"hell" or "punishment." What is at issue is not the fear of hell as
some imagined punishment imposed upon me by some vengeful being
more powerful than myself in return for my having done something
to "wrong" him. What is at issue, rather, is the sudden perception that
my life till now, my life lived in forgetfulness of God, *was* hell: that
hell is the same as life itself, lived without "God."

However, if I continue to let myself be driven forward by the fear
of lapsing back into such hell, what gradually happens to the alcoholic

in recovery also begins happening to me as the "repentant sinner." For the alcoholic, as I have said, the joy of living sober slowly replaces the fear of drinking as the dominant motive for continued abstinence. Where once the alcoholic crawled awkwardly along the path of recovery for fear of drinking again, the alcoholic now runs happily for joy of continuing sobriety. It is the same for me if I am driven toward God by fear of the hell of returning to Godlessness: as St. Benedict says at the end of his chapter on humility, by continuing patiently to climb the ladder of humility I will find, once I take the final step, that where once I ached with a gnawing fear of hell, I now am filled with joy in God. Where once I acted out of fear, I now act out of love.

It is in the love of God, according to St. Hilary, Benedict's predecessor, that my fear of God is brought to perfection: in love, fear is complete.

Self-Evaluation

Take a good look at your fears. Ask yourself honestly: What am I afraid of? Instead of reacting fearfully to fear itself by running away from your fears or denying them, take the time to listen to them carefully. What do your fears have to tell you about yourself?

- Review the four-column exercise from the "Disciplines, Practices, and Exercises" section at the end of the preceding chapter. There the four columns were used to look at anger, but they can easily be adapted for fear as well. In the first column, list one at a time whatever you are afraid of. In the second column, write exactly *why* you are so frightened by whatever it is you listed in the first column. Just what about that person or thing makes you so afraid? In the third column, look at what aspects of your life you feel are affected by each frightening item from column one, as focused in column two. Finally, in the fourth column ask yourself how you contribute to your own fears. What traits in your own character open you up to your fears? (Perhaps low self-esteem subjects you to fear of making new personal contacts, for instance. Or maybe a lack of trust in others makes you afraid of getting into situations where you may need to ask for help.)

Disciplines, Practices, Exercises

If you want to lessen the hold fear has on you, it is the fourth column of the fear inventory just discussed that tells you what you most need to know. It is precisely by addressing those traits of character that show up in the fourth column that you can do the most to alleviate your own fears. The two exercises that follow focus on helping you do that "fourth-column" work.

1. During your daily life, whenever an occasion presents itself in which you have typically felt fear in the past, practice acting *contrary* to the troublesome traits identified in the fourth column of your fear inventory — acting contrary to it *before* you actually begin to feel fear again, if at all possible. (For example, if lack of trust in others is one of your problems, you can make deliberate, recurrent effort to ask for help in not-yet-threatening situations where you don't even "need" the help at all yet.)

2. Follow St. Benedict's advice to remind yourself daily of your own mortality. Above all, whenever you begin to feel afraid, remind yourself that you are going to die. That reminder has a wonderful way of clarifying the situation and aligning priorities. When I actively remind myself of my own coming death, such things as what others think of me, or whether I get the promotion I want, suddenly lose importance.

– Five –

Humbling Pride

...to be humble is to walk in truth, for it is a very deep truth that of ourselves we have nothing good but only misery and nothingness.
— St. Teresa of Avila, *The Interior Castle*

My father died in a recent year, a few days after Thanksgiving. He was eighty-four years old. The last few years of his life he was in the advanced stages of Parkinson's Disease, complicated by the effects of a series of minor strokes. For the final two years before his death, he and my mother lived with us. She still does.

At least until Parkinson's stopped him, my father always led a very active life physically. Even into his mid-seventies, he would probably have been able to beat me in any test of physical strength, agility, stamina, or endurance.

Just over a year before he died, we took my father on his last family trip. Since long before I and my older sister and brother were born, he had liked traveling through the Front Range of the Rockies to the Western Slope of Colorado, to Glenwood Springs, where he enjoyed swimming in the enormous hot springs swimming pool for which the town is famous. We took Dad there one last time.

By then he was no longer able to do anything without help. He couldn't walk alone at all and could only take a few steps, very slowly, when helped by someone strong enough to hold him up when he tottered, as would inevitably happen. My mother's strength was no longer enough to keep him balanced. Only I or the visiting nurses we had hired to help keep him exercising within the limits the disease still allowed could walk with him at all. He couldn't even stand up alone, and when he occasionally slipped out of his chair he couldn't get up again by himself.

He could no longer feed himself, and even when others fed him he had trouble chewing and swallowing. Sometimes he just wasn't up to exerting himself enough to try. Then the food would just sit in his mouth until it finally all dribbled down his chin or someone removed it for him.

He drooled continually. One of the few ways in which he was still able to help himself was by mopping at his mouth with facial tissue wadded in his hand. He could no longer pull the tissue from the box. But if someone put some in his hand, he could, with effort, use it. Sometimes that effort was also too much for him. Then he would just sit there, drooling.

Nor could he any longer attend to his own bodily eliminations. Because of incontinence, he had to go back to wearing diapers, like an infant. Up to the very end, he still tried to let my mother, or whomever else was there to help him, know when he needed to relieve himself, especially for bowel movements. Then his care-giver had to help him into his wheelchair, wheel him into the bathroom, pull him up out of the chair again, and place him back down on the toilet seat. When he was done he could not clean himself. That, too, had to be done for him.

By the time we went to Glenwood Springs it also took tremendous effort for him to speak at all, so much as a single intelligible word. He rarely even tried any more.

At the pool in Glenwood Springs I took charge of pushing him in his wheelchair to the edge of the pool, then pulling him up and slowly lowering him into the warm water. He helped all he could, but for the most part it was up to me. Once in the pool, the water gave him enough support that he could stand by himself if he kept one hand on the wall, or if he leaned his back against it.

Despite his condition, my father was somehow still able to take pleasure in his own life. For example, when something he was being fed tasted good to him, he still showed it, if by no more than making extra effort to chew and swallow. He also still took pleasure in his youngest grandchild, my wife's and my daughter. He liked to watch her play, or have her talk to him, as she was always quick to do when she came home from school. They were special friends to one another, even — perhaps especially — under those difficult conditions; and the rest of us could still see the pleasure he continued to derive from her friendship.

He also liked being in the water of the hot springs pool on that final family trip. I could see it in his eyes and the relaxation that came over his face while he was soaking there, leaning against the wall.

His granddaughter was playing with a soft sponge-rubber ball, about six inches in diameter. She started throwing it softly to her grandfather. With his back against the wall and the water buoying him up, he was able to use both hands and awkwardly draw the ball toward himself. He would work it into his right hand, which he would then awkwardly try to lift toward his shoulder. Then he would slowly bring his arm forward, trying to toss the ball back. But his hand wouldn't obey him. It wouldn't let go. So he would end up just returning the ball, still clutched in his claw-like hand, back into the water. One of the rest of us would gently take it from his hand and toss it back to his playmate, and the game would begin again.

During the entire time my father wore a broad, delighted grin.

Not long after we took him out of the water after playing with that ball, my father needed to make a bowel movement. We had been careful to try to schedule our trips to the pool around what my mother had learned of his body's schedule. Before that episode, I had only had to help him urinate in the men's locker room at the pool. I didn't enjoy that task much, but it was still within the bounds of my emotional tolerance.

Although I had sometimes had to assist him at bowel movements at home, when I would spell my mother for a while, I had so far managed to avoid a situation in which I had to assist him in that way at a public facility. The prospect of having to do so now made me

THE PRIDE THAT NEEDS HUMBLING,
AND THE PRIDE THAT HUMBLES

There's a pride that won't let me ask for help when I need it. This is the pride of arrogance and self-importance. It needs to be humbled. Such pride actually hides a defensive uncertainty about myself, about my own worth.

The sharpest possible contrast to such self-important pride is provided by an altogether different sort of pride, the pride that admits and accepts even the most extreme dependence, weakness, and neediness with grace and dignity. This second type of pride does not need to be humbled. Instead, this pride itself does the humbling: when we encounter it, we are humbled.

uneasy. Even in the privacy of our home, the chore was one I found extremely difficult.

In the first place, my personal fastidiousness in such regards tends to be excessive. So does my discomfort in thinking about elementary bodily functions in my parents, whom I (in common with many middle-class American white children, at least) would prefer to think of as beyond such indelicacies. I felt embarrassment for my father in his position, and embarrassment for myself in my own. In addition, childish irritation at him for not being able to "control" himself tugged at me.

All of that is to be set against a background of what I had always perceived, at a very deep level, to be a long history of my father disgracing me in public by his behavior. Telling long stories, cracking crude jokes, hugging and kissing every woman he met, wise-cracking with salespeople — all those and more elements in my father's habitual behavior had given me innumerable occasions throughout my life to feel ashamed of him. Especially as an adolescent, I often felt embarrassed to be associated with him publicly. (Once again, of course, there are many others, at least of my class, color, nationality, and, perhaps, sex, who have had similar feelings toward their own parents.)

It was with no relish, therefore, that I wheeled him toward the men's room at the pool in Glenwood Springs. Mustering my resolve, I proceeded with the job of getting him into the wheelchair-accessible stall and hoisting him up and over onto the toilet. As he often did, he started to try to turn himself sideways on the seat. Such compulsive "trunk twisting" is common in Parkinsonians. After I corrected his position a few times, he finally settled down. I waited grimly for him to finish his business, which he eventually did. Then I helped him to his feet. Clinging to the bars provided on the walls of the toilet stall, he was able to hold himself semi-erect while I tried to clean him up. I felt at the limits of my tolerance and prayed that he could hold himself up long enough for me to finish, and not crumple into a messy heap wedged next to the toilet bowl, where I would have no easy time doing anything with him.

Although I told myself I "shouldn't," I felt disgust and anger toward my father for putting me in what I perceived as yet another awkward situation. That, in turn, gave me guilt for feeling disgust and irritation. More to myself than to him, I defended myself at one point by saying, "I'm doing the best I can, Dad."

As difficult as it was for him to do so, he struggled to articulate a reply. Although he went on to live for slightly more than another year, that was one of the last times my father ever spoke to me directly. "So am I," he said in a clear, moderate, accepting voice. I knew he was telling the truth. His pride was humbling.

Humility is not thinking less of yourself; it's thinking of yourself less.
– ANONYMOUS

Great achievements are not necessarily humbling. Nor are failures, great or small.

My own achievements tend to puff me up rather than humble me.

They make me full of myself, as someone who is cocky and boastful is said to be "full of himself."

On the other hand, the achievements of others tend to make me envious, not humble. They may, indeed, make me feel "down on myself," but not in a humbling way. Instead, the negative self-judgments occasioned in me by others' successes tempt me to search for ways in which I can, as it were, deny them the right to those successes. I look for all the ways in which they have been more fortunate — by birth, looks, class, connections, and so forth — than I have. I try to convince myself that, had I been half so lucky, I would have succeeded beyond them. It seems to me that I can build myself up only by tearing them down.

As the successes of others can depress me, so can their failures make me gleeful. Even though I may publicly express sympathy and support, in my heart I am all too often glad to see them fail. It makes me feel less of a failure myself.

As for my own failures, they tend to increase my defensiveness rather than my humility. The more I fail, the more I feel driven to boast of my accomplishments, in a usually futile, never more than temporarily effective effort to make me feel all right about myself. Or else I feel compelled to deny my failure, asserting my ability to succeed despite the evidence, like the active alcoholic dying of his condition while still proclaiming he can "handle" his drinking.

Thus, neither failure nor success as such is humbling.

Love is patient and kind; love has no envy; love doesn't exalt itself,
is never puffed up.   – 1 CORINTHIANS 13:4

However, simple love is often humbling. A dog wagging its tail seeking my pat just moments after I have irritably scolded him can bring me a sudden feeling of repentance that is humbling. Any such experience of being loved purely — loved neither for anything I have done nor for anything that I am, but simply loved, the same when I fail as when I succeed — is humbling. It leaves me with a reservoir of sheer gratitude from which I can continue to draw humility in the future, without ever exhausting the supply. It may at times be difficult, even nearly impossible, to find my way back to the source of such clear, cooling water, but it is always there somewhere.

Love builds me up. It "edifies" me. In one of his letters in Christian Scripture the apostle Paul writes concerning spiritual gifts that such gifts are given to those who receive them, not for the recipients' own sake, but in order to be used for the edification — the building up — of the entire church community. He also writes that, used with love, such gifts will always build up, but that they never will when used without love. That is one way in which the fruits give knowledge of the trees that bear them. Whatever builds up, comes from love; whatever does not, does not.

Love builds up the person loved. When I experience being loved, I am edified. I am built up. By building me up, love lets me become humble.

> *It was said of Abba Arsenius that when he was in the palace, no one wore finer garments than he, but that when he was in his cell living the holy life, no one was more poorly clad.*
>
> *– Sayings of the Desert Fathers*

The better I feel about myself, the less vulnerable I am to the kind of pride that takes the form of feeling that some things are "beneath" me. When, deep down, I feel good about myself, I don't mind doing even the most trivial, mundane, or unpleasant tasks, tasks I would otherwise find distasteful — too "dirty" perhaps; at any rate just not the sort of thing a person of *my* stature should be expected to do.

To be able to give up all pretense of being somehow "special," I have to be completely at home with myself. Not myself as I would like to be, but myself as I actually am, with all my defects and imperfections. I have to accept myself thoroughly, with all of my

LOVE AND HUMILITY

Love humbles us, and humility allows us to love in turn.

When we experience being loved, truly loved, we experience being affirmed "unconditionally." That is, we experience being held as precious and irreplaceable just as we are, with all our imperfections, limitations, and weaknesses rather than as some sort of reward for our supposed achievements or personal assets. It is humbling to experience oneself as loved in that way. At the same time, it is only because we ourselves receive such love, and are thereby humbled enough to let go of some of our self-absorption, at least for a moment, that we are able truly to love others in turn. To paraphrase something St. John says in Christian Scripture, it is only because we are first loved, that we, in turn, are able to love. Being loved humbles us enough to love.

limitations — all the ways in which I am petty, envious, possessive, insecure, cringing, cowardly, selfish, thoughtless, greedy, covetous, slothful, and resentful; my too large nose, my misshapen lips, the irritating drone in my voice, my middle-aged paunch, thinning hair, increasingly wrinkled skin, my flab and my fat and all the other things I dislike (or at least am less than delighted with) about my body; and all the other items in my physical, psychological, or emotional make-up I might wish were different. I have to accept myself with them all. I have to outgrow the desire to be different than I actually am, if I am ever to outgrow the desire to be different from others, "special" in some way.

To be able to let go of the sense that there is something special about me — that I am unique in some unique way, as opposed to the common way in which everyone is unique — I have to be perfectly humble. I have to be capable of finding happiness and joy just in being myself, without being anybody special.

Often, I still have too much of the wrong kind of pride to do that. Or perhaps I have too little of that other kind of pride, the kind I discerned in my father, when his simple acceptance of himself and his condition humbled me at the pool in Glenwood Springs. When it comes right down to it, I would still often rather be miserable than give up all sense that I am something special. In contrast, my father, as I experienced him during that episode at the pool, was proud enough that he could be content with happiness.

Traditionally in mainstream Western thought, humility has been taken to be the opposite of pride. I've come to suspect, however, that humility is less the opposite of pride than of insecurity about oneself.

Such personal insecurity often manifests itself in what today is called *codependency*, the need to be needed that so often *tears people down* (especially people who enter, or find themselves placed in, situations where they must be care-givers for others). But it is also just as likely to take the form of that disingenuous kind of pride that *puffs up*, without ever genuinely *building up*.

It is the person who is insecure about himself who feels the need to put on airs, brag of his accomplishments, and, in general, strive to "look" good in the eyes of others. For example, men who are insecure about their masculinity often mask their insecurity by adopting "macho" personas. The man who is truly at home with his own masculinity feels no need to parade it around in such ways. Nor is he (like the less secure man who may be quick to carry heavy loads to help out a woman, but who refuses to carry her purse, for fear of being seen with it) reluctant to do things that may appear to others as stereotypically "feminine."

Disingenuous pride exalts itself in order to escape insecurity. It is such self-*exalting* pride that needs to be humbled. In contrast, there is a self-*accepting* kind of pride. It is such self-accepting pride that does the humbling.

Aristotle says that every virtue is a mean between opposing extremes — extremes that oppose one another, as well as each opposing

PRIDE AS SELF-EXALTATION, PRIDE AS SELF-ACCEPTANCE

The pride that puffs up — the kind of pride that needs humbling — is the pride of self-exaltation. This is the sort of pride that is quick to take offense, always on the look-out for slights, protective of its accomplishments, and ever-attentive to differences that separate one out as somehow "special." It is the pride that makes us eager to call attention to ourselves.

On the other hand, there is the pride of simple self-acceptance. This is the sort of pride that has no need to call attention to itself. It is a pride which is so confident of itself that it no longer has to take offense at anything or ever worry about being slighted. This is a pride that delights in being nothing special. As for accomplishments, such pride is so sure of itself that it is no longer even conscious of having any accomplishments: such pride is so proud, it no longer needs to "accomplish" anything at all.

the given virtue. Humility is often falsely taken to be the mean between the extremes of "too much" self-love or self-esteem — too much "ego," in short — and "too little" of it. But in that sense of the term, *any* ego is too much, and there can *never* be too little of it.

Humility is not the "right amount" of ego ("just enough" ego, as it were). It is not the mean between too much and too little ego. Rather, humility is no ego at all. It is ego-less-ness, *freedom from* ego.

Humility is the mean between the extremes of self-exaltation and self-deprecation, *both* of which reflect investment in the ego. Humility is a mean which escapes each of those two extremes at once, by escaping the ego-centrism that supports both — the self-concern that goes with insecurity about oneself, as expressed either in exaggeration of one's merits or in exaggeration of one's lacks.

Humble people no longer need to be concerned about themselves, about trying to prove themselves — to themselves or to anyone else. They no longer need to be concerned with how they "appear." They need no longer be either self-*exalting* or self-*deprecating*, but are freed to become self-*accepting* instead.

The focus of their concern has shifted from themselves to that before which the self stands naked, stripped of the pretensions, either positive (self-exalting) or negative (self-deprecating), in which it attempts to wrap itself. As a friend of mine recently put it, humble people have come to realize, not just intellectually but also in their hearts, that no one ever really possesses anything except the breath one breathes moment by moment, and that even that breath must be *given* to one. They have come to realize that, of themselves, they are nothing. Humility reveals their own nullity to the humble.

On one hand, the revelation, in humility, of one's own nothingness, one's own nullity, burns away all claims of special individual merit and scorches the soil in which self-exaltation might otherwise grow. Thus, humility *casts down* those who would exalt themselves. On the other hand, humility is not self-deprecating, either. Instead, it *lifts up* those who have cast themselves down — or been cast down by others.

Humility is not the awareness only of *one's own* nullity, but also of the nullity of all others, rich and poor, powerful and powerless, famous and anonymous alike. It is the revelation of the ultimate nullity off all human endeavors — the vanity of vanities proclaimed in the book of Ecclesiastes from Hebrew Scriptures.

By relieving them of the necessity to put on airs of any sort, attempting either to exalt or to deprecate themselves, humility frees the humble to enjoy their own lives to the fullest. They are freed for accepting life itself as a pure gift, neither awarded for any supposed merit nor withdrawn for any supposed lack of it, but given freely to all (as the sun shines and the rain rains upon all, "good" and "bad" alike, according to Ecclesiastes).

Knowing the nullity of all endeavors to acquire "merit," save "face," or in any other way earn or preserve a high place for oneself, the humble are liberated from the double-mindedness that otherwise necessarily characterizes human action. So long as one is caught in the illusion of possible personal merit, whatever one does, one does it with only one eye on the goal of the action. The other eye is always cast toward the mirror, to see how one's action makes one look: Does it properly conform to, and confirm, the view of oneself to which one clings, either in self-exaltation or in self-deprecation? But the insight provided by humility dispels that illusion, restoring singleness of vision, purity of intention.

According to an ancient Christian tradition, the proximate goal of monastic life, for men and women alike, is "purity of heart." In the nineteenth century, Kierkegaard wrote an "edifying" (which is to say, literally, an "up-building") discourse on purity of heart. Kierkegaard was no monk, but his definition of purity of heart fits well with the monastic tradition. Purity of heart, according to Kierkegaard, is "to will one thing." At least by that definition, humility purifies the heart.

Self-Evaluation

How much of your pride needs humbling? That is, how much in you needs to be cast down? That question is one of two you should focus on to evaluate your own pride. The other question is, How much of your pride *is* humbling? That is, how much in you needs to be lifted up?

- You can simultaneously get an initial sense of how much of your pride needs humbling (that is, of how proud you are in the self-exalting sense of pride) *and* of how much you need to build up your low self-esteem by asking yourself one simple question. Both the need to exalt ourselves and the need to put ourselves down come from the same source: an underlying sense of *lacking* worth and personal dignity. Accordingly, you can get at the roots of both your self-exaltation and your self-deprecation by asking yourself a single question: "In what ways am I *defensive* about myself?"

Be as thorough as you can be. Then, once you've finished taking stock of all the things pertaining to yourself about which you are defensive, you can use your list to do the first exercise suggested below.

Disciplines, Practices, and Exercises

Here are three basic exercises for building humility.

1. Choose someone you have reason to believe will be receptive and supportive, ask that person to help you, then set up a meeting at which you share the list you have just compiled, the list of all the ways in which you are defensive about yourself. Ask the other person simply to listen to what you have to say, and then to pass along any insights or suggestions she or he may have, without trying to "fix" anything.

2. Be attentive to signs that you are becoming defensive about yourself; then whenever you notice yourself growing defensive, simply let go of your defensiveness.

3. Stop justifying your actions. Let them speak for themselves.

– Six –

Boredom: The Devil at Noon

"If you're bored, it's because you're boring."
– An Anonymous Alcoholic

That's what a young woman in Alcoholics Anonymous said to another AA member, an elderly man who was complaining to her about being bored at some AA meetings. I heard the story from him. To his embarrassment, he told me, he had had to acknowledge to himself that she was right: he was responsible for his own boredom; if he was bored, it was finally because he *chose* to be bored — and what is more boring than that?

Boredom is the choice not to care.

If I am bored, then that is because at some level I have made a choice no longer to invest myself fully in my current situation. To a degree exactly corresponding to my boredom, I have made a choice no longer to care. In that sense, I am always responsible for my own boredom.

In the European Middle Ages, the standard list of the so-called seven deadly sins included *acedia*. Medieval monastics called *acedia* "the noonday devil."

Roman hours did not correspond to modern ones. The "hours" of today are all of equal duration. No hour in the modern sense is either longer or shorter than any other. Every hour is exactly equal to every other.

In contrast, the Romans divided the daytime into twelve equal segments or "hours," then did the same with the nighttime. Thus, when the daytime was long, as it is in summer, each of the twelve daytime hours was considerably longer than each of the twelve nighttime ones.

112

That would reverse in winter, when the night stretches itself out to its maximum extent: then a nighttime hour became much longer than a daytime one.

The ninth hour was called "None," which is Latin for ninth, and from which the modern English "noon" derives. In summertime, the ninth hour of the monastic day actually corresponds to about 3:00 in the afternoon. Our "noon" — the point at which the sun is directly overhead, the middle of the day — occurred around the sixth of the monastic hours.

At any rate, it was above all in the middle of the day, beginning around the sixth monastic hour, then stretching beyond that into the afternoon, that *acedia* was most to be feared. The monastics' "noonday devil" was the tempter spirit set loose around midday, to roam freely in the afternoon.

You shall not fear the terror of the night, nor the arrow that flies by day; nor the plague that prowls in the darkness, nor the scourge that lays waste at noon. – Psalm 91

Acedia is usually translated as "sloth," but that is misleading. "Boredom" is a better translation, though even that is not quite right.

Today, the standard idea of "sloth" is that of laziness or indolence. The sort of image that commonly comes to mind for sloth is of someone lying in a hammock in the summer sun, snoozing, when the grass needs cutting, the garage cleaning, and the porch painting. Or the stereotype is that of an overweight man in a torn tee-shirt sitting in front of the television, drinking beer and watching football, while his untended responsibilities keep accumulating. The slothful person — the lazy, indolent person — is one who is always just sitting around wasting time rather than being usefully occupied.

The opposite of the lazy, slothful person, in turn, is the *busy* person: the man or woman who is always running around tending to something. She or he is the person who is always occupied, the one who is involved in all sorts of activities, serves on all the committees, and volunteers for all the functions; the person who is always tending to a myriad of things; someone who has no time at all to waste on napping in hammocks or sitting down to watch television (except, perhaps, for the occasional "educational" program — and even then usually only "for the sake of the children").

Ironically, however, it is precisely the "busy" person, and not the lazy one dozing in a hammock, who comes closest to exemplifying the sin of *acedia.* To push the two stereotypes — of the lazy person and the busy one — to their extremes: it is the workaholic rather than the bum who has been possessed by the noonday devil of the monastics.

That is not to say that the bum, the man snoozing in the summer sun, or the beer-guzzling football fanatic are examples of monastic or contemplative ideals. Far from it. They are just as bedeviled, just as lost in sin (to continue using the medieval terminology), as the workaholic executive, the overinvolved parent and neighborhood activist, or any other busy-ness addict. Nor are the sins of the lazy and indolent any less deadly, less deadening — less soul and spirit enervating — than the sins of the men and women who never have any time to spare.

It is just that *acedia* is not particularly the sin to which the bum, the overage day-dreamer, and the football junkie fall prey. Greed, gluttony, pride — above all an eighth sin (the original lists had eight, rather than seven, deadly sins), the sin of sadness — all play a role in sloth, indolence, and laziness. But *acedia* is not a major factor.

Acedia is the impatience, the restlessness, that chafes against whatever is long and long-drawn-out. It is rebellion against whatever is routine and repetitious, whatever is all of one color or all of one sound: the monotonous (mono-tonous: one-toned). It is the voice whispering in the ear that, when there are so many interesting, exciting, fun, distracting, entertaining, inviting, diverting, important, productive, practical, and/or worthwhile things to do, it's foolish to waste one's time on dry, boring, monotonous, mundane, pointless routine.

Acedia is boredom. It is the restlessness that can come over a person engaged in anything that requires patience and the endurance of monotony.

This is a harsh, terrible demon, always attacking the monk, falling upon him at the sixth hour, making him slack and full of fear.... He suggests to the monk that he should go elsewhere and that, if he does not, all his effort and time will be wasted.

– John Cassian, *On the Eight Vices*

Mornings in a contemplative monastery tend to be relatively busy times. The monastics must rise early, in the dark, well before dawn, shaking off sleep to go to the chapel for the first of seven daily periods of community prayer centered around the chanting of the psalms from the Hebrew Scriptures. Then come (though not necessarily in this order): breakfast, three more periods of chanting in the chapel, daily Mass, a period of reading and study, regular morning chores, the beginning of the daily work period, and the second meal of the day. All of those activities are packed into the morning hours of the day, filling it with things to do.

Even if some of the activities of the morning — for example, the long period of chanting right after rising, which is the longest of the seven daily periods of common prayer — become monotonous after a while, the sister or brother knows that it won't be long before that activity is over, and a new one comes along. But then comes the long afternoon. During the afternoon, there is work to be finished, to be sure. And there is more reading and study to be done, if one wishes. But throughout the afternoon there is no meal to break the monotony, and there is only one prayer service. That takes place in the ninth hour of the monastic day, and it lasts only for about fifteen minutes; so it doesn't give much relief. All that the brother or sister can do is try to hold on until the bell rings for Vespers, the sixth period of common prayer (from Latin for "evening"), signaling the end of the afternoon, the beginning of the end of day.

Then evening comes. Evening is full again, like the morning. In the evening there is Vespers, then a final meal for the day, a period of community recreation, a brief community reading, and then Compline, the prayer service to end the day. After Compline there is time to oneself, then bed and the night's sleep.

Thus, the other two parts of the monastic day — morning and evening — are lively enough, relatively speaking. But, oh, those afternoons.

Acedia, the devil to whom the afternoon belongs, is boredom. It is the temptation to choose not to care — the choice that engenders in me an insatiable craving for the new.

> *To detach our desire from all good things and to wait. Experience proves that this waiting is satisfied. It is then we touch the absolute good.*   – SIMONE WEIL, *Gravity and Grace*

The Buddha knew that mere experiences of pleasure or displeasure, no matter how intense, were not of themselves sufficient to create craving. For craving to arise, one must not only experience pleasure or pain, but choose to act upon the experience in a certain way. The choice so to act, the Buddha taught, was itself grounded in ignorance: one made that choice only because one didn't know any better, in effect. The fact that the choice was made in ignorance, however, did not make it any the less a choice.

Craving itself can take either of two forms, depending upon whether the experience occasioning the choice from which the craving arises is a pleasant one or an unpleasant one. If the experience is

ACEDIA: THE TEMPTATION TO BE BORED

The monastic vice of *acedia* is still very much with us to-day. Put simply, *acedia* is the temptation to be bored — that is, the temptation to give up on what one is doing, because one is finding it "boring," and to go off in search of distraction, instead. No sooner does something become "routine" for us than we begin to experience this temptation. We begin to grow restless and listless. We get a yen for new places and new faces — for anything "new," anything, that is, other than what we are doing, that has become so routine, so "boring."

That term — *boring* — captures the quality of the experience at issue quite well. In *acedia*, or boredom, we feel as though we are being hollowed out: *Acedia* bores into us like a drill, boring us out, leaving us with a gaping hole bored clear through the very middle of us.

pleasant, then one will crave to hold onto that experience, to prolong it for as long as possible, and then to seek it again, once it is over. On the other hand, if the experience is unpleasant, then one will crave to escape from it, to have it end as soon as possible, and then to avoid any recurrence of it, once it is over.

The liberating insight that the Buddha had into the interconnections of pleasure, displeasure (or "pain"), and craving was that one did not *have* to take the step from the experience to the craving. Instead, if only one chose to do so, one could simply sit back and experience the experience, without trying either to prolong and repeat it, if the experience was a pleasant one, or trying to escape and avoid it, if it was unpleasant or painful.

There's a common misunderstanding among all the human beings who have ever been born on this earth that the best way to live is to try to avoid pain and just try to get comfortable.

             – PEMA CHÖDRÖN, *The Wisdom of No Escape*

Monotony is unpleasant. At times, it is downright painful.

I remember long afternoons in school. School was always monotonous for me, all the way from kindergarten through college. At times, it literally became excruciating.

In kindergarten, before my teacher wised up to what I was doing, I would go up to her desk and tell her I was sick to my stomach (which was certainly true enough) whenever the pain of the monotony got so bad I felt I just couldn't stand it any more — that I *had* to do something to escape it. She would send me to the nurse, who would call my mother. My mother would then come and get me and take me home. The relief was immediate.

Unfortunately, my kindergarten teacher eventually caught on to what was happening. Then she blocked that particular escape route. So I had to find others — at least I thought I had to. In my ignorance, I didn't know any better. And my teacher was too ignorant herself (or too vicious, which is unlikely) to enlighten me.

You become a narcotics addict because you do not have strong motivations in any other direction.   – WILLIAM BURROUGHS, *Junky*

Years later, I discovered that cigarettes were an easily available, invariably reliable way to escape the pain of monotony. Smoking is an excellent diversion. All the smoker has to do is light up and inhale deeply. Then there is plenty to attend to — to get interested in. The spectacular effects of nicotine upon the body's nervous, pulmonary, and cardiovascular systems give the smoker endless opportunities to explore. All the body's resources are called upon, just to monitor the changes and maintain some sort of balance.

When one first starts smoking, the internal confusion induced by the intake of nicotine is so great that just maintaining basic coordination is as much as one can handle. Of course, the body eventually (actually, relatively rapidly) adjusts to the presence of nicotine in the system. But once that happens, the smoker can still find countless hours of relief from boredom just in closely monitoring, mostly through unconscious processes, his or her body for signs of nicotine depletion, then replenishing it as necessary to maintain a constant level.

BOREDOM AND ADDICTION

Boredom, more precisely, the endeavor to *avoid* boredom, is a major factor in addiction. By its very nature, an addiction fills up the addict's time. Distraction, diversion, in short, escape from boredom, is always available to the addict. All an addict needs to do to find all the diversion and distraction anyone could ever want, at least for a moment, is to take another drink, smoke another cigarette, get another fix — or even just set about "trying to score."

The escape from boredom plays a tremendous, but so far all but unexamined, role in the genesis of addiction, not only to nicotine but to other drugs from alcohol to heroin, as well as in nonchemical addictions such as workaholism. Even if contemporary consumer society did not push drugs and addictive processes on its members, it would still generate a potentially limitless market for them through the relentless monotony of daily life in such a society, coupled with the total refusal of that society to provide skills, models, and education for coping with boredom in *healthy* ways.

Although it would be years later before I started to smoke, in a very real sense my kindergarten teacher set me up eventually to become an addict (if not to smoking—and alcohol—then to some other substitute). By failing to teach me positive ways of responding to monotony, while simultaneously blocking my access to *natural* means of escaping monotony (calling on someone responsible for my well-being — namely, my mother — to get me out of there!), she left me, in my ignorance, no alternative.

I do not blame my kindergarten teacher for the fact that I became an addict. I don't blame her, because I know that she was acting in ignorance herself. Her intentions, I have no doubt, really were all for the best; she really was doing what she did "for my own good," so far as she could see. Nevertheless, she is among those responsible for my eventual addictions.

For me the twelve years between the time I was forced to endure the numbing monotony of kindergarten and the time, as a senior in high school, that I discovered alcohol and nicotine, was a period characterized by nine-months' yearly of five-days-a-week torture. I hated school. There is no other word for it.

Already as a child I knew what it was like to spend all my Sundays in depression because I knew that Sunday meant Monday was coming again, just tomorrow. Friday and Saturday were the good times, when Monday seemed so far away that it would never come. But Sunday was merciless. I didn't have to wait until I grew up and had to go to work at some job I hated to see that side of Sunday.

When I finally did discover alcohol and tobacco, it was no wonder, then, that I embraced them passionately. They appeared to me as a deliverance.

For twenty-four years of dedicated drinking and smoking I was unable to see through that appearance. Only then did I see that, in reality, both were servants of the same devil that likes to haunt monastic noons.

The importance of advertising... does not lie in its manipulation of the consumer or its direct influence on consumer choices. The point is that it makes the consumer an addict, unable to live without increasingly sizeable doses of externally provided stimulation.
    – CHRISTOPHER LASCH, *The True and Only Heaven*

The prolongation of enforced monotony in combination with the proliferation of readily available diversions that is so characteristic of contemporary life is a systemic evil within consumer society. It is a systemic, societal dimension of the reality that Christians experience by the name of "sin." It creates a general atmosphere in which the pursuit of diversions from boredom becomes compulsive for ever larger numbers of persons. Such addictive need, in turn, creates and sustains an ever growing market, awaiting further exploitation. Precisely because addictive needs can never be satisfied — there is never "enough" for an addict — a population of addicts is the ideal market for a consumption-based economy.

Christian teaching today, especially in the Roman Catholic church, emphasizes that what Christians call sin is operative not only at the level of individual choices and decisions, but also at the level of social institutions, and even — in some way that can be experienced far more easily than explained — at the cosmic level, the level of the cosmos as a whole. Nor can sin at one level be separated from sin at the other two levels. In some crucial way, individual, societal, and cosmic evil interpenetrate and enable one another. For example, the sinful choices of the individual have, in reality, a more than individual impact. They carry a weight which drags down not only the individual who sins, but also the society of which the sinner is a part, and even the entirety of creation. In Adam, to use an ancient formula, all humans fell, and with them the whole cosmos; and Adam continues to fall each time a single person today falls prey to temptation and "sins."

The systemic sin of consumer society whereby prolonged, enforced monotony is conjoined with the marketing of an unending array of diversions from that very monotony creates a genuinely *diabolic* situation. That is a situation in which the individual is continually *provoked* to sin in his or her individual choices. The individual is "provoked" to sin in the etymologically literal sense of being called out into sin, being challenged to come forth into it. The individual is provoked into personal sin in the same sense that a schoolyard bully keeps provoking a weaker child to a fight. The bully keeps on provoking the other child, calling that other child names, pinching him or her, poking fun, and so forth. The provocation continues until the weaker child at last gives in and tries to fight back. Then, when that finally occurs, the bully can proceed to beat and humiliate the other child, which is just what the bully wanted all along. The bully can beat and humiliate at will and even in perfectly "good conscience," since, after all, the weaker child has now "asked for it."

Consumer society provokes consumers to commit the sin of choosing no longer to care, no longer to struggle against the seemingly insurmountable monotony of the life such a society imposes on its members. The provocation is relentless and continuous, until the individual finally gives in.

To give in to that provocation is actually to go ahead and do what one is being provoked to do. It is actually to go ahead and to *choose no longer to care.*

BOREDOM, THE PURSUIT OF DIVERSION, AND CONSUMER SOCIETY

Modern consumer society institutionalizes compulsive pursuit of diversion as a reaction to boredom. In other words, it institutionalizes addiction. What matters is not *what* consumers are addicted to, just so long as they are addicted to *something*. It is the compulsive pursuit of diversions as such, regardless of the specific form that pursuit may take, that keeps the engine of consumer society running.

When I choose no longer to care, I can no longer endure the monotony. I must go in search of diversion. I begin to look around for something *interesting*. The "interesting" is what grabs my attention. It is what "entertains" me. The interesting is the opposite of the monotonous.

When I give in to the provocation of boredom, of *acedia*, by going in search of the interesting, I drive the boredom away. At least that is how it seems to me: that I have driven it away. In truth, however, it is simply that the boredom has now achieved its goal. The devil has done his work and is now free to move on to new challenges. He has provoked me, and I have not been able to withstand the provocation; I have given in and done the very thing he was provoking me to do. Alternately worded, the devil of boredom has tempted me, and I have yielded to the temptation.

And once I yield, I become all the more yielding. It becomes all the easier, the next time I am tempted, to fall prey to the temptation. Furthermore, my threshold of provocation, as it were, is lowered each time I give in and do what I am provoked to do. In the future, it will take less to provoke me to that point of giving in, less to tempt me beyond my limits to resist.

The interesting is never interesting enough. Its promises are false. When something interesting initially grabs my attention, it promises to *keep* me interested. But even the most interesting thing soon loses its interest, as in the old idea of how dispiriting it would be if Christmas came every day — even though children wish it would.

At the heart of the interesting is a vacuum. It is the vacuum created by the departure of care — the sort of care, of choosing to continue to care, that alone can empower someone to endure the monotony of tending to a parent or spouse with Alzheimer's disease, for example, or remaining faithful for a lifetime in a marriage, or honoring monastic vows. The interesting is what can still appeal to me, even after I have chosen no longer to care. But precisely because there is no more care on my part to sustain the interest, the whole weight for keeping me interested falls upon the interesting thing itself, which must now work at an ever increasing intensity to hold my attention.

The interesting can remain interesting only by continually changing, continually offering something "new." Accordingly, it is no wonder that contemporary commercial civilization, based as it is upon the attempt to escape boredom through the institutionalized pursuit of the interesting, is characterized by an ever more rapidly expanding proliferation of novel diversions, of "leisure activities." The new is never new enough.

The attempt to keep boredom at bay by seeking diversion doesn't just fail; it is counterproductive. It makes boredom worse. The *more* diversions individuals or societies possess, the *greater* the boredom. The two, diversions and boredom, vary directly with one another. They are mutually reinforcing. There has surely never been a society more bored than advanced commercial society today, a society in which the number of diversions readily available to all segments of society is already at a record high, and keeps on growing. Nor, surely, has there ever been a more boring society than this one.

"If you're bored, it's because you're boring."

To be boring is to have chosen no longer to care. It is to have yielded to the provocation, the temptation, of boredom, and thereby to have been taken in thrall to — literally to be "en-thralled" by — the "interesting." And now, once enthralled, I become a servant of the very devil I think I am escaping by pursuing all my diversions, a servant of the devil of boredom. Now I spread boredom myself, wherever I go.

I become the one who must always be entertained. The one who cannot sit still for a genuine conversation or to read a challenging book (serious writing often eschews all effort to entertain, and thereby loses "interest" for those not able to endure monotony). The one who can't endure a long lecture, no matter how deep and intense, learned or enlightening. In short, I become the average modern consumer, always demanding something new, always on the lookout for "bargains."

The more energetically I seek to escape boredom through the pursuit of diversions, the more susceptible to boredom I grow, and the more boring I become. If the cycle is to be checked and reversed, I must at last cease fleeing from boredom, attempting to exorcize it with the "interesting." I must, instead, turn *toward* my boredom. I must *embrace* the very monotony from which I have suffered, suffered so acutely that I could not withstand boredom's provocations any longer and gave in to the temptation not to care any more. I must continue to care, despite all the monotony of caring.

LEARNING TO LIVE WITH BOREDOM

As with other distressing emotions, such as anger or fear, to cultivate boredom, and allow myself to be cultivated *by* it, I must do the very opposite to what the emotion itself invites me to do. I must break my natural reaction to boredom, which is to seek to escape it by finding diversion. I must substitute a response of turning *toward* boredom rather than reactively turning *away from* it and into distractions.

For better than a decade, a movement has been growing to overcome the obvious failings of the American educational system from kindergarten through graduate school by making school more "interesting." Today, the "cutting edge" of that endeavor lies with the utilization of contemporary computer technology. The basic idea already found excellent expression in the 1970s in *Harry Stottlemeier's Discovery*, the first of a series of novels at the heart of the Philosophy for Children program created by Matthew Lipman. At one point in *Harry*, one of the characters — Mark, a middle-school student who is highly intelligent and no less highly bored with school — remarks that there is no reason such really important things as history shouldn't be presented in ways that attract and hold students' interest. TV commercials are devised to make trivial things like soap look appealing, Mark says, so why shouldn't the same apply to the subjects taught in schools? Why shouldn't classes in history and English be packaged with as much commercial flare as the latest dish detergent, for example?

I certainly understand Mark's anger and frustration. I felt the same way throughout my own school years. However, what looks to him like a solution is really, I think, just more of the problem. It seems to me that the remaining chapters of *Harry* — and the subsequent novels that Lipman has written for the Philosophy for Children program — make clear that what Mark really needs is not some form of commercialized education, but the support of a community of friends (what Lipman would call a "community of inquiry") that upholds Mark in his frustration and boredom and empowers him to rise above them. What Mark needs is just what Harry and his other friends end up giving him: a safe place where he is allowed to express his emotions and confront them.

The point is certainly not that school should be made more boring, in some sort of an attempt to force the issue. That would be spiritual adventurism. School is already far more boring than it needs to be. To that extent, Mark's complaint is justified, and efforts to remedy the situation by encouraging more creative, less standardized ways of presenting classroom materials are to be applauded. The point, however, is that emphasis should not be placed on making school more "interesting" by devising ever more diverting modes of presentation. It should be placed, instead, on making schools into the sorts of communities represented by Mark, Harry, and their friends. That is, emphasis should be placed on encouraging students to face boredom and learn healthy ways of responding to it.

With boredom, as with all the so-called negative emotions (all the emotions that are unpleasant, and from which one therefore tends to flee, such as anger, fear, and shame), the only way out is through. The escape from boredom begins only when one ceases to try to escape it.

Schools can learn from contemplative monasteries. One of the wonderful things about monasteries is that they provide places where escaping from boredom by pursuing diversions is made difficult. By the secluded setting, by the silence, by the daily routine of monastic life, even by the colors on the walls and the arrangement of the buildings, one is gently but insistently encouraged to cease denying one's boredom, and to embrace it.

When asked how to become holy one desert hermit in the early centuries of the Christian church replied simply, "Stay in your cell. Your cell will teach you everything."

One of the things my own "cell" — that is, my own spiritual practice or discipline — has taught me over the years since I turned forty and began to learn how to feel is to handle my boredom gently. I have learned that boredom is a guest that will not ever be driven away, but will cheerfully depart of its own accord if I just abide with it for a time. How long a time that will be I never know in advance. That is up to the guest to determine — without impatient urging from me to keep the visit short.

Not only will the devil of boredom leave in due time if I just refrain from trying to drive him away. He will transform himself before my eyes from a devil into an angel, a messenger of God, come to bring me glad tidings. The glad tidings boredom brings me — the gift boredom leaves me, if only I cease refusing to accept it — are that monotony itself, in the last analysis, is no more than an illusion, a veil that must be parted to see the truth.

John Main, the English Benedictine monk who taught the "Christian meditation" that I practice daily, once told the story of how a young man who was visiting at the monastery expressed amazement that monastics were expected to remain in the same place, even the same room or cell, throughout the remainder of their lives. The young man wondered how they could stand it. How could anyone stand every morning waking up to the same old view out the same old window in the same old cell, to face always the same old daily routine, repeated day after same old day through all the weeks, months, and years? How could anyone live a life in which nothing new ever happened?

John Main's reply was that it was in the very sameness of each day, and each moment of each day, that the committed monastic eventually

EDUCATING FOR BOREDOM

One thing lacking in contemporary schools, from kindergarten through graduate studies, is education for boredom. That is, at no level of their education are students given any positive role models of how to embrace routine and monotony rather than fleeing from it into the compulsive pursuit of diversion. Students are also given no tools for confronting their own boredom, no sense of their own responsibility for it, no useful information about alternative approaches, and, above all, no training in facing and transforming their own boredom through patience and endurance. They are just left to their own devices in confronting the deadening monotony that goes with years of sitting in class.

found the greatest variety. It was in the very sameness of the view each morning that the monastic discovered the absolute irrepeatability of *this* view, *this* morning.

The new is never new enough. Only what is always the same can be always new. That is why all basic forms of meditation or contemplative prayer, whether coming from Christian, Buddhist, Hindu, or other traditions, are based upon *repetition*. There is the repetition of some word, as in Hindu *mantras*, for example. Or there is repetition of some motion, as in the "whirling dervishes" of the Islamic Sufi tradition. Or, as in Zen sitting meditation, there is simple attending to one's own breath, with its continually recurring cycle of inhalation and exhalation.

The wisdom of the world's various meditation traditions is that it is only through embracing such apparently monotonous repetition, in which the same old thing keeps happening time after time after time, with never a moment's break, that one can finally "escape" boredom. The craving for the new, the interesting, and the diverting is an insatiable craving — as the Buddha knew all craving to be. Only monotony has the power gently and slowly — by sure but virtually imperceptible steps — to wear that craving down, and finally to extinguish it altogether. And only then can one begin to live freely, basking in all the rich abundance of each and every moment, regardless of how ordinary and "uninteresting" it may be. Only then does one truly begin to *live* one's own life rather than just trying to live through it.

Too many of us never manage to do more than merely to survive our lives. We need to learn to live them. That is why we have been given monotony as our teacher.

A year or two ago, a good friend and I made a retreat together at the Monastery of Christ in the Desert, in the Ghost Ranch region of northern New Mexico. On Sunday afternoon my friend had a talk with one of the brothers, who gave her a wonderful definition of monastic life. Monastic life, he said, was "creative monotony." *Creative monotony:* That phrase is appropriately redundant.

Self-Evaluation

Where do you encounter boredom in your own life, and how do you react to it? Here are two approaches to take in answering that question. Use both of them.

1. Review your experience with boredom over the years. Ask yourself such questions as: What typically bores you? When were you most bored in your life so far? Next, examine how you react to boredom. Do you seek distraction? If so, how? Or do you just "tune out" (by going to sleep or going blank, for example)? Look for your patterns of reaction to boredom.

2. Review where in your life you invest the least care. Where do you tend to make things easy on yourself rather than throwing yourself enthusiastically into what you are doing? These points of weakest care are typically pressure points for boredom.

Disciplines, Practices, Exercises

Corresponding to the two approaches to evaluating the role of boredom in your life, here are two exercises for learning how to face whatever boredom you do experience.

1. Embrace boredom when it comes. That is, when boredom strikes, do *not* seek diversion, as boredom itself shrilly demands you to do. Instead, just sit there and feel your boredom. Explore it. Learn its texture. Watch the onset, increase, peaking, decrease, and eventual cessation of the impulse to seek diversion. That impulse will always go through all those stages, just as any other impulse does. Sometimes the impulse will pass quickly, sometimes it will take longer (it may seem like forever), but pass it always will, eventually. When it does, pay attention to what feeling or feelings replace it. (Sometimes, after the worst, most seemingly endless attack of "this terrible demon," as John Cassian calls it, you may feel a remarkable sense of calm and peace, as though having bored you hollow, your boredom has now left you completely refreshed and clean.) As with anger and fear, the only permanent solution to boredom lies in facing it squarely rather than running from it. Again as with them, you will also find that your capacity to stand and withstand boredom will increase, the more you practice this exercise. On the other hand, such "demons" are cunning; so you can expect there to be times that you seem to be getting worse rather than better. When that happens, just practice all the more diligently. The improvements will become obvious to you, over time.

2. Invest care. Whenever you notice that your are beginning to lose interest in what you are doing or what is going on around you, consciously make the decision to invest *more* care and concern, rather than less, in what is beginning to lose your interest. As you practice this exercise regularly over a long enough time, you will find your capacity to care expanding. You will become less passive in relationship to your own life and the situations in which you find yourself. Instead, you will become more a part of whatever is occurring. And you will also find that, without even trying to accomplish such a thing, you are less often beset by boredom.

– SEVEN –

Shame and Shamelessness

You ought to be ashamed of yourself.
– A MYRIAD OF VOICES

Like boredom or fear or anger, shame is commonly regarded as a "negative" emotion. Whatever else may eventually be decided about the wisdom of that terminology, at least in part it is based upon the actual experience of shame, since shame (like the other "negative" emotions) is an *unpleasant* feeling. It is not pleasant to feel shame.

Furthermore, shame can also easily appear to be negative in its consequences. That is true on at least two levels. First, it is true at the level of how one feels about oneself, the level of self-esteem, self-loathing, or self-acceptance. Second, it is true at the level of one's behavior, of how one acts in the world.

When I feel ashamed, it is often in a situation in which I don't feel good about myself. Indeed, in situations in which shame is common, I often feel downright bad about myself. I often feel self-doubt, self-disgust, or even self-loathing.

The consequence of being made to feel ashamed in such situations in which I am already unsteady in my self-acceptance or in which I am already actively disgusted with myself is that my self-doubt or self-disgust is only deepened. If I start out with self-doubt, the self-doubt tends to become self-disgust; and if I start out with the latter, it tends to become self-repulsion, and I begin to relate to myself as to an obscenity. If where I start out is already self-loathing, shame can push me over the line into complete despair of myself: I lose all hope *for* myself, along with any remaining traces of confidence *in* myself.

132

When I experience shame under such conditions of damaged self-acceptance, how I act typically reflects how I feel about myself. Either I act in self-destructive ways, trying to erase my shame by erasing what I take to be its cause: myself. Or I act in ways that are destructive of others and especially of my relationships with them: I "act out" my shame in aggression, struggling to assert myself against the current of shame.

Both ways of acting from shame are counterproductive. Instead of lessening my underlying shame, they increase it.

THE TRIPLE NEGATIVITY OF SHAME

In *The Merchant of Venice* Shakespeare says that mercy is "thrice blest." Well, shame, a merciless emotion, is "thrice cursed."

First, shame is one of what Aristotle called "distressing" emotions: emotions the feeling of which causes us distress. Shame is cursed because it is unpleasant or distressing.

Second, shame is cursed because of its effects upon the one who feels it. When we feel ashamed, our self-esteem and sense of self-importance are attacked and lowered. We are made to feel "ashamed *of ourselves*," as we aptly say.

Finally, shame is cursed because of its effects upon our behavior. When we feel "ashamed of ourselves," we are tempted to act out our shame either by doing things to hurt ourselves (for being such shameful and worthless creatures), or by aggressive behavior toward others, to cover our shame.

As with boredom, fear, or anger, the only way out of shame is through it. I must learn to cherish my shame, as Thich Nhat Hanh says I must cherish my anger.

To cherish my own shame is not to try to talk myself out of it. It is not to try to rationalize it away by convincing myself that I really have nothing to be ashamed of.

Everyone always has something to be ashamed of.

I am ashamed of what I am.

— JEAN-PAUL SARTRE, *Being and Nothingness*

Guilt, it is sometimes said, is the feeling that I have *done* something wrong, whereas shame is the feeling that I *am* something wrong. Using that formula, if everyone always has something to be ashamed of, that means that for everyone there is always some sense in which she or he *is* something wrong. Put differently, for everyone there is always some dimension or level of self at which, even if one has not *done* anything wrong, one still ought to be ashamed of oneself.

That is precisely why it is not possible truly to remove the feeling of shame by anything one does. Since the underlying feeling of shame in the first place is not based upon an assessment of anything one has done, but continues even when one has "done" nothing wrong, that underlying shame cannot be erased by any amount of activity. No amount of trying to do the right thing, or to do things right, will "fix" the feeling.

The hopeless "innocence" of modern man who is so full of sin that he no longer experiences contrition, and is consumed with guilt only for what is relatively inoffensive, is one of the most heart-rending mysteries of our time. — THOMAS MERTON, *The Inner Experience*

Authentic shame is the experience of *contrition*. In authentic shame one experiences contrition not for anything one has done as such, but *for being the way one is.*

SHAME AS THE SENSE OF "BEING" WRONG

Shame is the sense that somehow "there is something wrong with me" in a way that goes beyond anything I might ever be able to fix. It is the feeling that I somehow "am" wrong, regardless of anything I might have "done" (or failed to do).

As a rough way of characterizing an important difference, we can say that *guilt* is the sense that I have *done* something wrong, whereas *shame* is the sense that I *am* something wrong.

Shame is the feeling of being exposed or shown up in my radical "being" wrong.

Everyone always has something to be ashamed about, because everyone always has a "self." Shame is shame for being oneself.

I loved my fault, not that for which I did the fault, but I loved my fault itself. — St. Augustine, *The Confessions*

The evil that one does would not be so shameful if one didn't enjoy it so. In his *Confessions* Augustine of Hippo recounts a boyhood episode in which he and some other boys stole some pears. What made the episode indelible in Augustine's memory was *why* he stole the pears. It was not from hunger or desire to possess. Augustine really didn't want the pears at all. What he wanted was to steal, that's all. He wanted to do wrong, solely for the sake of doing wrong. He wanted to commit a violation, just in order to violate. It was an act of pure ill will with no excuse.

Augustine's act of theft was petty in terms of the monetary value of what was stolen, or in terms of the loss to the owner of the pears, or in terms of the consequences of the act (no needy person was deprived of food because of the theft, for example). Nevertheless, that petty act of theft carried cosmic meaning. In that act, Adam fell again; sin once again entered the world.

And once again the taste of sin was sweet: Augustine liked it. He really, really liked it.

The way I am, speaking personally, is that there is something in me that hates innocence (unless it be the "hopeless," counterfeit innocence Merton mentions). I'm like Augustine: I need no motive for defiling what is undefiled; that it is undefiled in the first place is somehow an affront to me. Whatever is undefiled calls out something in me — something that *is* "me" — that wants to defile it.

Nobody sins inadvertently. Nothing makes one sin. One sins because one chooses to. Provocations or temptations merely offer convenient excuses for doing what one wants to do anyway. It's fun to sin. Not that fun things are sinful because they're fun. Rather, sinful things are fun because they're sinful. Take away the sin, and they aren't so much fun any more.

Authentic shame is contrition for being someone who takes delight in doing something wrong, solely for love of the wrongness of it.

One would rather will the not, than not will.
— FRIEDRICH NIETZSCHE, *Genealogy of Morals*

What in various traditions is called "sin" has nothing to do with breaking some moral or legal code. It is not a matter of acting contrary to orders, not a matter of rebelling against some authority. Instead, to quote Merton in *The Inner Experience* again, "The sense of sin is then something ontological and immediate which does not spring from reflection on my actions and comparison with a moral code. It springs directly from the evil that is present in me: it tells me not merely that I have done wrong, but that I *am* wrong, through and through."

AUTHENTIC SHAME

As opposed to everyday, inauthentic shame, which focuses on how I look in the eyes of others, authentic shame focuses on an aspect of how I truly am, in my own deepest experience of myself. Authentic shame is the concrete disclosure to me of that aspect of myself that takes perverse delight in what is harmful, either to myself or others, solely because it is harmful. In the concrete, to become aware of myself *as* being that way is simultaneously to experience contrition *for* being that way. Accordingly, authentic shame can also be defined as such contrition: to be ashamed of myself authentically is to be moved to contrition for being the way I am, insofar as I am someone who takes pleasure in the harmful as such.

I *am* wrong. I am wrong, not at the level of any attributes or traits with which I find myself born or pick up along my way. Whatever those characteristics may be, and regardless of whether they are inherited or acquired, there is always a fundamental sense in which I am *not* those characteristics. I can always draw a distinction between myself and them. I "have" them, to be sure; yet they can never really define me.

If I *am* wrong, "through and through," that cannot be at the level of such characteristics. It must be at a deeper level, the one beyond characteristics and (therefore) beyond characterization, the level where only the bare word *I* remains. It is the level at which I — for no one else does it for me, surely — make the basic choice of myself, the choice that "I" *be*, apart from and beyond all my traits and attributes. If I am wrong through and through, it can only be at that level of the pure choice that I be, that I myself *be*, and that I be *for myself.*

How can I "be" wrong — "be" wrong at the very deepest level, where I choose myself to be in the first place?

The anonymous fourteenth century author of *The Cloud of Unknowing*, a classic of Christian mysticism, writes that only that person knows "genuine sorrow" who realizes not only "what" one is but "that" one is. That remark suggests that genuine shame, the shame of knowing that one *is* wrong, through and through — the sort of shame that elicits the genuine sorrow to which the author of the *Cloud* refers — comes from recognizing that one *is* in the first place. If that is so, then what it is to choose to be *wrong*, through and through, is simply to choose to *be* at all.

That is, to choose not only to do wrong but to be wrong, at the very heart of oneself, is to choose to be a "self" at all, in the sense of a being who asserts his or her own existence as separate and apart from other beings. To *be* wrong is, according to that way of experiencing it, to be as the self-assertion of oneself apart from others.

At the end of his *Genealogy of Morals* Nietzsche writes of the will that would rather will nothing than not will anything. That is the will that prefers actively to will destruction, annihilation, and violation rather than to relinquish itself as will. It is the spirit of "If *I* can't have it, then no one can have it; I'll destroy it first," the spirit of "If I can't have things *my* way, then I'll see to it that nobody else has it her way, either." It is *self-will* in the most literal sense: will as pure self-assertion, pure willfulness.

Genuine shame is the sudden and shaking revelation that nothing, absolutely nothing, is more important to me than myself, and having my own way. It is the shocking recognition that "I want what I want when I want it," regardless of what anyone else wants and regardless of the consequences — and the recognition that that's exactly how I want to be.

Here is the opening stanza of one of the poems of Gerard Manley Hopkins:

> As kingfishers catch fire, dragonflies draw flame;
>   As tumbled over rim in roundy wells
>   Stones ring; like each tucked string tells, each hung bell's
> Bow swung finds tongue to fling out broad its name;

Each mortal thing does one thing and the same:
Deals out that being indoors each one dwells;
Selves — goes itself; *myself* it speaks and spells,
Crying *What I do is me: for that I came.*

That is a perfect description of hell. And the real hell of it is, that's just where I — where we each — want to be. What a shame.

Very often the parental attitude serves to inculcate in the girl a sense of shame regarding her appearance. . . . This feeling of shame leads the girl to act awkwardly and to blush incessantly; this blushing increases her timidity and itself involves a phobia.

– Simone de Beauvoir, *The Second Sex*

John Bradshaw and other contemporary teachers have popularized the idea of "toxic" shame. Toxic shame, as the name implies, is poisonous to those who feel it. It poisons them against themselves.

What's toxic about toxic shame, it seems to me, is not the shame. It's the shaming. More precisely, its the shamelessness of the shaming.

Authentic shame is a pure gift. It is the gift of sorrow not only for what I am, but for the fact that I am at all, to speak with the author of the *Cloud.* It comes as a revelation, a sudden burst of light illuminating my own existence to myself. It cannot be imposed upon me any more than can any other gift. It can only be offered. It is always up to me to receive or refuse it.

In contrast, what is called "toxic" shame comes to me not as a gift but as an intolerable burden. It is imposed upon me. It is the product of acts of shaming inflicted upon me by others (or by myself acting as a surrogate other).

"You ought to be ashamed of yourself," someone tells me. The implication is that I'm not already. Most of the time the implication is correct: in fact, I do not especially feel any shame. Since I have just been told I ought to feel it, however, that part of me that believes what others tell me about myself (and there is always such a part of me) is ashamed that I don't. Thus, the other person's declaration that I ought to be ashamed of myself makes me feel ashamed of myself. It *shames* me, even if I have done nothing wrong, and even — indeed, especially — if I have no sense of *authentic* shame at all.

Shaming imposes "toxic" shame upon me. Others can shame me, or I can shame myself for them. But shaming, whether from others or from myself, can never bring *authentic* shame down upon me. In fact, authentic shame inoculates me, as it were, from being shamed.

When struck by authentic shame, I am brought to know that not only nothing I do but also nothing I am — none of my attributes, let alone my actions — can truly shame me. If it is true that I "ought to be ashamed of myself," that is never just because of my character, however vicious, or my behavior, however criminal. It is because I *am* at all.

Filled with shame at the very fact of my being at all, I have no more room to be ashamed of myself for what I do or fail to do, for who I am or fail to be. No one can shame me any longer, not even myself. I realize that no number of reprehensible traits or actions could ever equal in reprehensibility the shameful fact at the root of my genuine shame: the fact of my self-assertion in being at all. That is my radical shame, in the literal sense of a "root" shame: a shame at my very roots. Such root shame uproots all other shame. The weeds of "toxic" shame cannot grow in the same soil.

At the same time that it inoculates me in that way from being shamed, authentic, radical shame restrains me from engaging in any shaming on my own part. It blocks me from shaming others or even myself. In the light of the recognition of the absolutely shameful fact that "I" *am*, all other offenses pale into insignificance. In the light cast by radical shame, what otherwise looks so shameful shows itself really to be nothing to be ashamed of. All those other shames are thoroughly relativized. Riven by my own ultimate shame, I can no longer strike toxic shame down upon myself or others. I am bleeding too profusely.

AUTHENTIC SHAME AND "TOXIC" SHAME

What is often called "toxic" shame is a shame which is imposed upon me by others. It is the sense that I do not measure up to some set of arbitrary social or personal standards — the sense of shame because of how I look, or talk, or walk, or the like. It is indicative of the *shaming* which others (parents, siblings, peers, "the authorities," society in general) have inflicted upon me.

In contrast, authentic shame is shame for my *self*, for the perversity lurking in my own deepest recesses. It is contrition for that perversity, a contrition that actually frees me from concern with arbitrary standards imposed upon me by others. In the light of the malice that lies coiled in my own heart, concern with how I look or what others think of me pales into insignificance.

Thus, authentic shame is actually an antidote to "toxic" shame.

Shame splits us down the center. Being split down the center is not particularly pleasant. So we flee from shame.

Insofar as the flight is involuntary — a conditioned reaction that operates contrary to one's own choice and will — it paradoxically delivers fugitives from radical shame over to being shamed by who and what they are. That is, it delivers them over to relative, "toxic" shame. It subjects them to the constant underlying sense that there is something wrong "with" them, something for which they owe ongoing amends, amends that will never be "enough."

Such involuntary flight from shame relegates one to a state of "shamelessness" in a nonpejorative sense. Nonpejorative shamelessness is based upon an ignorance for which the shameless person bears no blame. It is shamelessness as a *burdensome lack* of shame — burdensome to the shameless person herself. As an antidote to such nonpejorative shamelessness, genuine shame brings one out of one's ignorance and liberates one from all toxic shame: one is liberated by shame from shame. Gifted with genuine shame, I realize that there is nothing wrong "with" me, such that there is anything I could ever do to "fix" it. There is nothing wrong *with* me; *I* am wrong "through and through," as Merton says. So there is nothing to fix. There is only myself, and the freedom to change, a freedom first shown to me — and thereby first really made available to me to exercise — in my genuine shame at being the way I am, through and through.

On one hand, then, there is this shamelessness of a nonpejorative sort, based on an involuntary ignorance that elicits flight from shame. On the other hand, however, there is all too often an element in the flight from radical shame that is *not* involuntary. The double negative is necessary here: "not involuntary," that is, not *contrary* to my own will, even if it is not something I consciously and deliberately choose — which latter would be the "voluntary" in the full sense. For example, in doing a good deed I may not have the intention of ingratiating myself with my peers. However, I am not averse to such an effect if it does occur. In the same way, to flee from radical shame may not be something a person consciously and deliberately chooses to do, but it is too often not contrary to the desires of those who find themselves in such flight.

To the extent that flight from radical shame is not involuntary it leads, not to a blameless sort of shamelessness that takes the form of a subjection to being shamed by others, but to a *blameworthy shamelessness* that inflicts shame on others. This blameworthy shamelessness is shamelessness in a pejorative sense. It is the sort of shamelessness at issue when someone is said to be a "shameless liar," for example.

To be shameless in this pejorative sense is to be not involuntarily in flight from shame. It is to be lacking in shame not because one has simply not yet been offered the liberating gift of shame, but because one *refuses* the gift (refuses it, in most cases, even before it is ever offered, in fact).

In his novel *Adventures in the Alaskan Skin Trade* John Hawkes defines "stupidity" as *willful* ignorance. Using that definition, shamelessness in the first, nonpejorative sense could be said to be based on simple ignorance, but only shamelessness in the second, pejorative sense could be said to be based on stupidity.

INNOCENT SHAMELESSNESS/ SHAMEFUL SHAMELESSNESS

If someone is shameless — lacking a sense of shame — that may be simply because that person is still innocent of authentic shame. Such a person would not yet have experienced his or her own malice, or, therefore, the contrition that goes with such self-experience. Shameless through no fault of their own, so to speak, those who are innocently shameful show nothing wilful in their lack of shame. It is as if their own wilfulness were still dormant within them. Accordingly, those who are shameless in this innocent way never try to impose shame on others.

It is the mark of shameful shamelessness, on the other hand, that those who are shameless in this second way *do* try to shame others. In fact, it is precisely there that their shamefulness lies: without shame — that is, without any sense of contrition for their own wilfulness — they self-righteously inflict shame on others. This is "shamelessness" in the negative or pejorative sense.

To be shameless in the pejorative sense is not only to be stupid; it is also to be shaming. When I shame someone, I shame that person for things that of themselves carry no shame, but that *I* would make shameful if I could. I treat what is only at most relatively shameful — shameful only if and insofar as it is indicative of the underlying wilfulness at issue in radical shame — as though it were shameful in itself, regardless of its relationship to root shame.

Stupid shamelessness is stupid precisely because it does not *want* to know genuine shame. The stupidly shameless person *wants* to remain ignorant of the wilfulness at the root of his person. Indeed, he must constantly *protect* himself from coming to know his own genuine shame. The best way to do that is by shaming others: shaming others makes the stupidly shameless person appear to himself as superior to those others. It makes him seem to himself blameless, precisely where it seems to him that they are to blame. To shame others is, therefore, to affirm oneself at their expense. However, self-affirmation regardless of its effect upon others is the very offense at the root of all genuine shame. Accordingly, by shaming others the stupidly shameless person, in the end, only adds to his own shame. As is true with all action based upon stupidity (*willful* ignorance), in the end shaming only makes things worse: the more one person shames others, the stronger grows the shamer's own root sense of shame. In short, willful ignorance is not only willful, it is also ignorant.

Stupidity is stupid. If it weren't for sheer arbitrariness, no one would tolerate it.

Self-Evaluation

Of what are you ashamed? Sort out your authentic shame from your "toxic" shames. Here are three suggestions:

1. Make a list of what embarrasses you; then consider the shame that goes with that embarrassment. Most of the time, feelings of embarrassment are pointers to areas of "toxic" or inauthentic shame. Authentic shame is inseparable from the feeling of contrition, of sorrow over what is sick and distorted in me. However, if I am genuinely contrite over something, then to that degree I am not *embarrassed* by it — I am *sorry* for it.

2. What are the things you have done in your life of which you are ashamed, and, more importantly, *why* are you ashamed of them? Is it because they cast you in a bad light, in one way or

another? If so, the shame is "toxic." Or are you ashamed through a genuine guilt of authentic shame?

3. When you feel shame, what do you *do?* Do you try to "cover" yourself, either literally or metaphorically? If so, then the shame is probably inauthentic, toxic.

Disciplines, Practices, Exercises

One exercise is designed to diminish "toxic" shame; the other to increase authentic shame.

1. Stop "covering" your shame. When you feel inauthentic shame, resist the impulse to hide your shame. Instead, just observe the impulse to cover yourself; don't yield to it, but also don't try to push it away; just feel it, and let it pass at its own speed.

2. Seek contrition as a gift; then accept it as one when it comes, giving thanks for it.

– Eight –

Sorrow, Sadness, and Depression

... the joy of unfulfilled desire full of promise, the joy of newfound possibility. – JOHN S. DUNNE, *Love's Mind: An Essay on Contemplative Life*

It is two days after Christmas as I begin to write this chapter. This year, as has become traditional in my family, I prepared dinner for us all on Christmas Eve, and we spent the evening together. Then on Christmas Day we opened presents, before another family meal in the afternoon. After it was all over, our daughter, who is going on thirteen, affirmed again something she has said often before. She told us that, as much as she enjoys Christmas Day itself, she prefers Christmas Eve.

That remark tells me that my daughter may be, as I am myself, more a creature of Advent than of Christmas itself. In the liturgical year of the Christian church, Advent is a time of preparation prior to Christmas. Advent is my favorite time of the year, and it has been ever since I was a child myself, long before I ever thought of taking being a Christian seriously.

The best time is a time of waiting. That is why the time before Christmas is the best time of the year for me. It is the best time of the year because it is the time most filled with waiting.

Especially for a Christian, Advent is a time of waiting and awaiting. During Advent the Christian awaits "the coming of the Lord." The word "advent" comes from Latin for "coming to or toward." Advent, in Christianity, is the season of Christ's coming to humankind. Especially in Christian mystical tradition, the coming of Christ is actually threefold. First, there is the historical coming of Jesus to be born to Mary, which is celebrated on Christmas Day. During Advent, Christians await the Holy Day of the remembrance of that historical birth. But there is also the coming of Christ that is promised for "the end of time" — the "second coming" of Christ, as it is commonly called. Awaiting the celebration of the historical coming of Jesus to be born of Mary, Christians also await this eschatological ("of or pertaining to the 'end times'") coming of the resurrected Lord at "Judgment Day." Finally — and as the bridge between the other two comings — there is the coming of Christ in the Spirit here and now, today, to the heart of the believing Christian. This third coming occurs every time someone awakens to the reality of his or her own condition — every time someone "comes to" herself or himself, as the Prodigal Son in the gospel story finally comes to himself and decides to return home, where he belongs and will be accepted in love.

The "proclamation of faith" that belongs to the celebration of the Eucharist in, for example, the Episcopal church (to which I belong) is also three-fold. For instance, the form from Eucharistic Prayer B, Rite II, in the Anglican-Episcopal *Book of Common Prayer,* begins with "we remember his death," then continues with "we proclaim his resurrection," before finally ending with "we await his coming glory."

That formula corresponds exactly to the threefold coming prepared for during the season of Advent and celebrated during the season of Christmas. First, "we remember *his* death" — the death of that very one who was born to Mary in the "first coming." Second, "we proclaim *his* resurrection" — the resurrection of that very same one, a resurrection through which that one continues to reign in our hearts today. Third, "we await *his* coming glory" — not the coming glory of some other one, but the "second coming," the eschatological advent, of that same one who was born to Mary and died on the cross, yet already lives again now.

Furthermore, the one whose *death* Christians remember during the period of Lent culminating in Good Friday, the day for remembrance of Christ's crucifixion, is the same one whose *birth* we await during Advent and celebrate at Christmas. If Christians don't remember *that* fact, then, despite their profession of faith, it is not "his" death they are remembering at all. Furthermore, to reverse the thought, if they do not remember the death on the cross that lies ahead for the baby whose birth they celebrate at Christmas, then it is not really "his" birth they are celebrating, either.

Yet, although as a matter of creed they live in remembrance of the death of that one, Christians are told not to search for that one "among the dead"; for, they are told, that very one whose death they remember is "risen." When some of the women who were among his first followers look in the tomb where he was buried on the first Easter morning, they are told he is "not there." He is, instead, alive in them, and in all other Christians, no matter how distant in time from that first Easter, in the Spirit that is sent into their hearts. The resurrection which Christians "proclaim" is not something that happened only once, long ago, and then was forevermore over and done with. It happens again each time a heart of stone softens and gives birth to the Word.

What is more, the very way in which Christians both "remember" the death of the crucified one who was born to Mary and "proclaim" that very one's resurrection now is by "awaiting" the coming again "in glory" of that same one in eternity, at "the end of time." It is right that the proclamation of faith ends and culminates with the affirmation that the life of Christian faith is a life of continual *awaiting*. In that sense, the entire life of the Christian is to be lived as though it were always the season of Advent.

Truly to wait is to hold oneself steady in an attitude of awaiting that which is already on the way, that which is already coming and the arrival of which is imminent, due at any moment, liable to break through and catch us unprepared if we are not careful. To wait is to await the arrival of what is on the way, and it takes great care. That is why waiting is always filled with *sorrow*, always *care-worn*.

THE SORROW IN ALL WAITING
AND LONGING

Waiting can itself be joyful. It is joyful whenever our waiting is filled with hope and anticipation, whenever we long for the arrival of what we are awaiting, and long for it in the certainty of its being already on the way.

Nevertheless, even the most joyful longing is also full of sorrow. Indeed, the greater the longing, not only the greater the joy of the anticipation of the arrival of what we await, but also the greater the sorrow, the pain, of the waiting itself. The very fact that we must wait, that what we await is not yet here, even though we are ever so certain of its being already on the way to us, fills us with sorrow that what we await is not yet here.

Longing as such carries sorrow in its core.

Yet waiting is also joy-filled. To wait, to await, is already to have what one is so care-fully waiting for. In waiting, we already receive in advance, as it were, the gift we are awaiting. In our sustained anticipation of its coming, the gift keeps giving itself to us in advance, even before it has ever arrived.

Indeed, perhaps gifts are more purely and irrevocably *given* in such anticipation than they ever can be in their actual presence. It is in our longing for the not-yet-present gift that we not only make ourselves *ready* to receive it (what is already full has no room to receive anything, it must be emptied first) but even most fully *do* receive it. The gift of all gifts — the gift *in* every gift — is granted not to grasping possession, which is at best momentary, but to patient waiting, which endures. Coming toward us, being on the way to us, a gift gifts us, by its very absence, with longing, opening us to receive.

I abandoned and forgot myself,
Laying my face on my Beloved;
All things ceased; I went out from myself,
Leaving my cares
Forgotten among the lilies.

– ST. JOHN OF THE CROSS,
"One Dark Night"

In Twelve Step groups every year, as the holiday season approaches, there is talk of how important it is for recovering alcoholics, addicts, and codependents to let go of their "expectations" concerning the upcoming holiday. For one thing, of course, expectations set us up for disappointments. If we don't expect anything, then we don't run the risk of failing to have our expectations met. Furthermore, if we approach the holidays with expectations about how things are supposed to go, we will tend to try to manipulate and control situations so that our expectations will be fulfilled. Since others don't like being controlled and manipulated any more than we like it ourselves, such behavior is all but guaranteed to lead to frustration.

As a rule, the greater our expectations, the greater the chance that they will not be fulfilled, and the greater, therefore, the likelihood that we will be unhappy. In short, expectations prime us to be unhappy when, as often happens, those expectations fail to be met.

Expectations also prime us to be unhappy when they *are* met. Indeed, the unhappiness of having our expectations met affects us at an even deeper level than the unhappiness of having our expectations frustrated. The unhappiness of *un*fulfilled expectations still lets us harbor the illusion that we would be happy if only our expectations were to be met. But the unhappiness of *fulfilled* expectations deprives us even of the solace provided by such an illusion.

I remember an old "Dennis the Menace" cartoon from my childhood. Dennis is sitting on top of a mountain of toys. Wrapping paper and ribbon are strewn all over the place. Mom and Dad are standing

THE SADNESS IN EXPECTATIONS —
BOTH MET AND UNMET

To have an expectation is, in effect, to set up conditions
to which I demand that the future conform. Inevitably,
however, expectations turn out to set *me* up for a fall.
Either I will find my expectations frustrated by a recal-
citrant future that refuses to conform to my wishes. Or
I will find my expectations fulfilled, only to be left with
a hole where my desire used to be. When my expectations are fulfilled, my desires are merely "satisfied." They
are "sated." And I am left feeling like someone who has
overindulged on Thanksgiving turkey. Nothing is more
saddening than such mere sating of desire and the inevitable sense of disillusionment that comes from having
all our expectations met.

by, observing the mess. No doubt they have been hoping to receive the
fruits of their labors in the pleasure that Dennis, they think, will show
in his new playthings. Their faces, however, display consternation, as
Dennis asks, "Is this all?"

Any halfway serious addict or alcoholic knows the feeling. Even
when all one's expectations have been fulfilled and more than fulfilled — indeed, *especially* then — it is not "enough." It is never
enough. "Is that all?" we ask ourselves, once we finally have all the
things we've dreamed of for so long, whether those things be material
possessions, honors, spouses, children, or whatever. "Is *that* all there
is?" Well, if so, then (as Peggy Lee sings in an old song I have always
easily identified with) let's break out the booze.

Success can drive one to drink as surely as failure, and perhaps more
rapidly.

Suffering does not necessarily mean sadness.... Sadness is a closing in upon oneself and it's placed very close to bitterness. Suffering is not that way; quite the opposite, suffering can create in us the space for solitude and growth in depth of character.

— Gustavo Gutiérrez, "Reading St. John of the Cross
from a Latin American Perspective"

The word "sad" comes from the same root as "sate." That is significant. Sadness, in fact, is the inevitable attendant upon satiation. The more satisfied I become, the sadder I grow.

Only hunger truly satisfies. Satisfaction only saddens.

That relationship between desire, the satisfaction of desire, and sadness holds true across the board of our desires. It is no less true of the hunger for sex than of the hunger for food, no less true of the thirst for reputation than of the thirst for water — or for wine.

Indeed, it may well be that one of the reasons wine is such a popular thing for thirsting after is precisely the more wine one drinks — speaking for myself as an alcoholic, at least — the greater one's thirst for it grows. That is, it may well be precisely the fact that consumption of wine or its equivalent (beer, whiskey, liqueurs, Sterno, etc.) *never* really slakes the alcoholic's thirst for alcohol that draws alcoholics to it in the first place: for alcoholics, drinking alcohol not only keeps the thirst for alcohol alive, but even increases it. If alcohol were able to satisfy alcoholics, there'd be no more reason for us to drink it; it would become as insipid to our taste as water.

For me during all my years as a "practicing alcoholic," drinking alcohol allowed me to postpone satisfaction indefinitely. From the first time I drank enough to experience the effects, I knew that alcohol was the thing for me, because I knew right away that I could never get "enough" of the stuff. That was precisely what attracted me to it: I realized that my appetite for alcohol was insatiable; it would never be satisfied.

I also suspect that at the heart of the success of the Twelve Step approach to getting souses off the sauce is this: the Twelve Steps teach alcoholics to substitute the thirst for God for the thirst for alcohol. Well, God is even better than alcohol when it comes to denying satisfaction.

"Sad," as I've already noted, comes from the same root as "sate," and sadness comes from satisfaction. Sorrow, on the other hand, comes from care.

A year or two ago I read an article in *Spiritual Life,* a Carmelite quarterly journal of spirituality, by Gustavo Gutiérrez, the Peruvian priest and theologian who is one of the founders and leaders of liberation theology. One remark in particular stuck in my memory, a remark Gutiérrez made in the context of a discussion of the poverty and suffering that is so much a part of daily life for so many people throughout the world today. Gutiérrez says that *suffering,* even the constant suffering that accompanies grinding poverty, is not incompatible with *joy.* Only *sadness* is, he writes. What he says of suffering in general certainly applies to sorrow as a form of suffering.

I thought I could describe a state; make a map of sorrow. Sorrow, however, turns out to be not a state but a process. It needs not a map but a history.   – C. S. Lewis, *A Grief Observed*

Advent teaches the same lesson about sorrow, suffering, and joy that Gutiérrez does. That has been brought home personally to me and my family during the past few years. For us, Advent has become not only a time of waiting for the holidays to come, but also a time of waiting for death. I will mention only two of the deaths that have come our way during recent advents, the two that affected us with the deepest sorrow.

Four years ago, my father-in-law died of cancer a few days before Christmas, when he was only seventy years old. He died in the living room of the house he'd lived in for almost fifty years, only three doors down from the house he had been born in himself. When he died, he was surrounded by his family, including me, my wife, and our daughter. The Christmas tree stood, lights aglow, at the foot of his bed.

Then last year my own father died a few days after Thanksgiving. He too died at home — our home. For him, it was a relatively new home, since he and my mother had only moved in with my wife and daughter and me two years before, after forty-nine years in the same house fifty miles away. My father, too, died surrounded by his family; and he too died with the lights of a Christmas tree (which I had made a special effort to put up early) shining over him.

Both deaths are painful losses to me and my family, yet both are also great gifts to us, adding a richness and significance to Advent that will only deepen with each passing year. It is not despite being painful losses that they are great gifts, but because of it. Remembering those deaths during the season in which they occurred renews the sorrow of our loss, but none of us would wish to be without that sorrow.

None of us, that is, would like to forget those two losses we have suffered. We want to remember the two fathers, grandfathers, husbands we have lost, and it is precisely our sorrow that tells us we do continue to remember them. How, then, could we be happy without our sorrow? If we did not have it, it would mean that we had forgotten — and how could we forgive ourselves for forgetting?

"For I, who am the Infinite God, wish to be served by you with infinite service, and the only infinite thing you possess is the affection and desire of your souls." – St. Catherine of Siena, *The Dialogue*

The great ascetics of all the world's various religious traditions knew well the lesson Gutiérrez repeats: the lesson that joy and happiness do not at all require the absence of sorrow. Indeed, under certain circumstances (for example, that of significant loss, such as the death of loved ones) joy and happiness even require its presence.

SADNESS AND SORROW

Sadness and sorrow are not at all the same thing. In fact, they are opposites. Sadness is the heaviness that comes from being sated, from being drained of all longing, all desire. It is incompatible with happiness and joy. But sorrow is a pain that lies even at the heart of longing itself, and is by no means incompatible with happiness, even joyful happiness. Sorrow is a state of suffering, and — as Gustavo Gutiérrez, for one, has pointed out — joy and happiness can coincide with even extreme, grinding suffering. There is never an acceptable excuse for intentionally creating or prolonging suffering, but suffering itself does not preclude deep, inner, joyful peace — a peace, indeed, that "passes understanding."

When, however, is anyone *not* in such circumstances? Who, after all, has not suffered significant loss? Even newborn babies have suffered loss, perhaps the worst loss anyone ever suffers, if certain psychological or psychoanalytical ideas are to be given any credence: the loss of the paradise of the womb.

"Asceticism" is, in effect, the art and discipline of cultivating desire. It is, therefore, also the art and discipline of cultivating sorrow. Ascetics are those who have discovered the secret to joy, the secret that joy can only be found *in* sorrow, and never in the attempt to escape from it. "To increase your joy, embrace your sorrow. To arrive at the peak of desire, deny yourself all satisfactions; only then will your joy be complete." That, in effect, is the meaning of asceticism.

When Lawrence Freeman finally decided to become a monk, he went to his spiritual mentor John Main (the teacher of the Christian meditation that I practice, as I have mentioned before). The latter asked the former if he was ready. The younger man thought the older was referring to all the deprivations and difficulties of monastic life, and he answered that he was resigned to accept the hardships involved in becoming a monk. "No, no," responded Father John. "I mean, are you ready to accept the *joy* of it?"

Since, then, those who know what is good by nature desire participation in it, and since this good has no limit, the participant's desire itself necessarily has no stopping place but stretches out with the limitless.   – Gregory of Nyssa, *The Life of Moses*

The satisfaction of desire sates and saddens. Only unsatisfied desire enlivens with joy. To satisfy a desire, to give in to it, is actually to try to drive it away. As discussed in an earlier chapter, fear, for instance, insistently baits us to reject it — baits us to try to drive the fear itself away either by running from what frightens us or by trying to fight and subdue it. Just so does desire in general always beg, in effect, to be reviled.

"Feed me!" cries my hunger, like the flesh-eating plant in *The Little Shop of Horrors*. But when I do feed my hunger, then, like the plant, it only grows hungrier, demanding ever more loudly to be fed even more. My hunger thinks it wants to eat, and it is not shy about telling me that's what it thinks. And the more I feed it, the more it thinks it wants to eat.

But my hunger is wrong. It doesn't really want to eat. What it really wants is something else. What it really wants is to hunger.

The one limit of virtue is the absence of a limit.
                        – Gregory of Nyssa, *The Life of Moses*

Jacques Lusseyran was permanently blinded by an accident when he was eight years old. "Despite" his blindness — more nearly because of it, and the heightened development of vision of another, intuitive sort it occasioned — a few years later, when he was only fourteen, he became a leader of the French resistance against the Nazi occupation forces during World War II. Eventually, he was betrayed to the Nazis. He then survived eight months at Buchenwald, one of the most notorious concentration camps, until he was liberated at the end of the war.

One of the gifts Lusseyran's blindness brought him was an absorbing appreciation for music. Throughout his life, music brought him great joy. Yet he is quite clear about music being no *pleasure* for him. In his autobiography *And There Was Light* he writes: "How can people call music a pleasure? Pleasure satisfied impoverishes and saddens, but music builds as it is heard."

Sorrow builds. It grows and grows.

Sadness passes with time, but sorrow only grows stronger. I felt the sorrow of my father's absence this Christmas more deeply than I did last Christmas; and if I can just keep out of my own way, I'm sure I will feel his absence even more deeply next Christmas. That is a solacing thought. It brings me hope.

Sorrow builds in another sense as well: it builds up those who suffer it; it "edifies" them. It strips away trivial concerns and vacuous pleasures in order to grasp and develop the heart and core of the person. Sorrow exercises the soul. "No pain, no gain."

Sorrow also builds community. By strengthening me and opening me up, it lets me experience greater understanding for the sorrows of others. Sorrow draws me into an open community of all who suffer, regardless of the comparative "objective" differences in the severity of the losses they have suffered. Those who have been subjected to great personal loss yet who have let their sorrow grow, rather than stifling it with resentment, anger, and denial, become *less* concerned with comparing their loss to the losses of others, not more. Having grown great in sorrows, they have also grown great in compassion, so that they can offer understanding, love, and support no less to the

SORROW AS EDUCATOR

If we let it, sorrow, when it comes, can be a great teacher. It can teach us acceptance, humility, patience, heightened appreciation, and even gratitude. If we let it, sorrow will also deepen our compassion and strengthen our sense of community with others. We need not seek out sorrow to learn the lessons it has to teach us. Enough sorrow always comes our way on its own, unbidden. All we need to do is to be open to it when it does come.

child crying over the loss of a family pet than to the parent crying over the loss of a child. Sorrow identifies; it doesn't compare.

Because it is unconcerned with comparison, sorrow also has no need to inflate itself, to puff itself up. Since sorrow builds naturally, it doesn't need to build itself up out of proportion, trying to call attention to itself.

In contrast, sadness is never sad enough. It always inflates itself; it always compares. There is always something of a preening actor — a "ham" — about sadness.

The twentieth-century French existentialist philosopher Jean-Paul Sartre wrote well about that aspect of sadness. In *Being and Nothingness* he discusses how we must literally "make ourselves sad." We put on our sadness as an actor puts on a part. We *enact* sadness.

I recognize clearly in my own behavior what Sartre is talking about. When I am sad, I do not *want* to be happy. If I catch myself slipping out of sadness, I positively yank myself back into it. Sadness is an image of myself that I actually work to maintain. I *want* to *appear sad*, not only in the eyes of others but also in my own. Hence, I carefully monitor my own demeanor, exaggerating signs of sadness and quickly stifling any signs that I may not really be as sad as I am trying to look. For example, if someone says something funny I may find myself distracted from my sadness for a moment. A smile may begin to form on my face, a chuckle in my throat. No sooner do I notice what is going on than I wipe the smile from my face and choke off the laugh in my throat. After all, I'm *sad!* How would it look for a sad-sack like me to be caught grinning and giggling? That wouldn't do at all.

Such behavior contrasts sharply with what can be observed among those who are suffering genuine sorrow. For example, a family gathered together by the death of one of its members will often move from crying to laughing at a moment's notice when someone recalls some humorous trait or escapade of the one who has died. Such mixture of tears and laughter is characteristic of genuine sorrow.

Sadness parades itself and wants attention. It seeks to perpetuate itself, refusing the very offers of consolation it insists others extend. In contrast, sorrow turns inward. It seeks only itself, and is quick to accept whatever comfort others are able to offer. Whether it is mere sadness or true sorrow, the cliché that misery loves company is true. But the reasons are quite different in the two cases. Sadness loves company because it wants to be seen and loses all meaning if deprived of an audience. Sorrow loves company for the healing it brings.

We are creatures of sadness because we are preoccupied with ourselves and how we look, what image we project. It is a matter of preserving appearances, of maintaining one's reputation. Only those whose basic desires have already been met have time to concern themselves with such trivia. Sadness is a privilege of the rich — or at least of those who are well enough off to have time to kill. Thus, beneath sadness, which might be said to be a sorrow of mere surface, there lies, paradoxically, an actual *insouciance,* which literally means "freedom from care." But to be free of care means to be free of sorrow. So the superficial sorrow of sadness disguises a hollow core of sorrowlessness.

To be without sorrow is to be without care. It is no accident that the English word "sorrow" comes from the same root as the German word *Sorge,* the translation of which is "care." Whoever cares, sorrows. And the more one cares, the greater one's sorrow. As the heart becomes gentler, more compassionate — that is, more caring — it experiences ever more deeply and cuttingly the injustice, pain, and suffering that it sees around it. At the limit of the development of compassionate care would be a heart that experienced the slightest suffering of another, no matter how distant and unrelated by natural ties, as an exquisite personal torture. It would bleed profusely at the slightest cut to the least of that universal humanity with which it had come to identify itself.

But once one sees and understands the possibility of such a thing, how could one choose to be anything less? How could one be satisfied with any lesser sorrow? Indeed, wouldn't the very longing to be so completely vulnerable (which literally means "wound-able"), coupled with the recognition that one is *not* yet that way, become itself a kind of torture? The soul granted such a desire — a desire to desire — would be *stricken* with it. It would pine away with grief for its very lack of grief, dying of the sorrow of its own sorrowlessness.

What a joy, surely, to feel such sorrow; how sad, never to feel it. Yet what resolution, what courage, such sorrow would demand. One would have to give up everything for its sake.

And that is a depressing prospect.

What we often tend to forget, however, is the preparatory grief that the terminally ill patient has to undergo in order to prepare himself for his final separation from this world.
>   – ELISABETH KÜBLER-ROSS, *On Death and Dying*

I have noticed that alcoholics and other addicts in recovery often find themselves going into a depression around their seventh year of sobriety. In my experience, the "seven-year depression" is no less common among alcoholics and addicts in recovery than is the proverbial "seven-year itch" among the married. At any rate, my own depression came along on that schedule.

Depression is very different from sadness. It is not something one seeks to perpetuate. It is not an image one strives to protect. The

SORROW AND CARE

To open ourselves to caring — to caring about others, ourselves, our work, or our play — is also to open ourselves to sorrow. The more we care, the more we expose ourselves to sorrow.

But think of the alternative! The only way to avoid all sorrow would be never to let ourselves care about anything. It would be never to care at all. However, no longer to care at all about anything is to develop a heart of stone. It is to become walking dead.

Furthermore, once we actually experience the compatibility of sorrow with joy — that sorrow can lie at the very heart of joy itself — the fact that caring opens us to sorrow will no longer count as any reason against caring. Instead, we will find the sorrow in caring only draws us on to care even more. The sorrow in caring will only make caring all the more precious to us.

---

secret pleasure one can take in being sad is altogether absent from depression. Those who are depressed do not at all wish to be.

On the other hand, depression is also different from sorrow. It is not the experience of painful loss, but more nearly the experience of the loss of pain — the experience of no longer being able to feel pain at all any longer, or anything else of intensity. It is a sort of deadness to feeling, an inability any longer to work up the energy to feel much of anything, except just tired. One of the common symptoms of depression is inordinate sleeping — or else inordinate wakefulness. Either one seems unable to do anything but sleep, or else sleep — at least peaceful, restful sleep — seems to be the thing one is least able to do. Whichever applies, one just can't get past the feeling of exhaustion.

The novelist William Styron and others have written detailed, moving descriptions of what it is like to suffer from depression. There is no reason to duplicate their efforts here. But I want to share one insight my own bout with depression gave me, an insight that connected depression in my mind with sadness on the one hand and sorrow on the other.

In time (with help from counseling and medication, among other things), my depression lifted. So far, at least, I have had no recurrence. As I look back on it now, from the far side of the experience, it seems to me that I emerged from the depression a less sad, but more sorrowful, person than I was when I entered it. Somehow and at least somewhat, my depression weaned me from sadness to sorrow. Or, rather, the depression was itself a process — or the affective dimension of a process — of relinquishing the one and embracing the other.

My own depression came upon me precisely when I least expected it. It didn't come when things were going badly in my life, as I would have assumed. Things were going well in all the major areas of my life — indeed, probably better as a whole than they had ever gone before. I was successful in my work; my financial situation was good already, and there were more improvements on the near horizon; my relationships with family and friends were all running smoothly; I'd been off the bottle for seven years and off cigarettes for six; and no doubt in large part thanks to that last-mentioned item, my physical health was excellent. Furthermore, a new book I had written had just been published. In short, I had every reason to celebrate.

In fact, it was precisely during a celebration, a party to mark the publication of my book, that depression caught up with me. In the very midst of the party, literally while I was greeting the guests and accepting their congratulations with a smile, I suddenly realized that I had just run out of the last bit of gas. I felt desolate. Instead of pleasure at my success in seeing a new book into print, I felt intimidation at the prospect of even thinking of the book, let alone talking about it to all our smiling, happy guests. I remember somewhere in the back of my mind a voice kept repeating that all the publication of the book and my other "successes" meant was that now I'd have to start the whole process over and do it all again—write another book, teach another class, have another bunch of intellectual conversations, spend time with my family and friends, whatever. And I just didn't have it in me to keep it all up.

Or, rather, I *did* have it in me to keep it all up. I didn't know how *not* to keep on doing it all over and over again, in fact. That's exactly what I *would* do—inevitably. And that was precisely the thought that left me so desolate: that there seemed no end to "it"—to the repetition over and over again of setting goals, striving for them, attaining them, then setting new ones. There seemed no end to formulating desires and struggling to satisfy them, only to find that, even if one did succeed in satisfying them, still one could not rest, since right away new desires sprang up to take the place of the old ones that had now been sated.

Think, for example, of eating to satisfy hunger. No sooner is the hunger satisfied than digestion, which has started even before that, begins to create a vacuum into which new hunger will soon rush. The thought of it is enough to sour one on eating altogether.

The same applies to all the appetites, all the desires; and that is what hit me, at some deep level, the evening of my book publication party. I just grew tired of wanting, tired of it not merely when the wants went unsatisfied, but tired of it most especially when my wants were *met*, as they had been met and were continuing to be met in my own life at that very point.

I grew tired of all that wanting, but at the same time I saw that I could not get free of it. No matter what I did, I would continue to want. Desires would continue to form in me, like bubbles of gas in some fermenting juice. That's all I was, apparently: a "desiring machine," as the French "postmodernists" Gilles Deleuze and Felix Guattari like to say.

Being sad makes sense only so long as one can preserve for oneself the illusion that some sort of lasting, ultimate, "real" satisfaction of desire is possible. The illusion is that somewhere, sometime, if one just keeps looking for it long and hard enough, one can finally find, in effect, the one and only meal of all meals, the one great meal that will finally satisfy all one's hunger for ever and ever, and at last grant one rest from all the hungering. It makes sense to be sad — either sad about not having one's desires met, or sad because they have been and have left one asking if *that's* all there is — only if one can continue to persuade oneself that such a thing as "real," "genuine" satisfaction is at least possible.

When that illusion of some sort of ultimate, utter fulfillment is finally shattered, there is no longer any room even for sadness. Instead of sadness, which still has its solaces, all that remains is emptiness, and the depression that comes from knowing it.

Acceptance should not be mistaken for a happy stage. It is almost void of feeling.   – ELISABETH KÜBLER-ROSS, *On Death and Dying*

After depression, however, comes acceptance. At least that is so in the popular five-stage model of the grief process that first emerged from the work of Elisabeth Kübler-Ross with terminally ill hospital patients. Kübler-Ross found that those who are diagnosed with terminal illness tend to go through a sequence that begins with *denial*, the attempt to reject the diagnosis. After denial comes *anger*, followed by the stage of *bargaining*, during which the patient tries to negotiate a deal (with God, for example) to escape the illness. The breakdown of such negotiations ushers in the next stage, when the dying person at last has to face up to the reality of her or his condition. This is the stage where all hope of recovery, medical or magical, is finally abandoned. The death of hope gives birth to the *depression* characteristic of this stage.

Depression, however, is not the last stage of the process. Rather, the depression, borne with, eventually gives way to the final stage, that of *acceptance*. Now the dying person accepts the inevitability of death — and paradoxically begins to live again. No longer absorbed completely with his or her illness, the dying person once again has time and

DEPRESSION AND SADNESS

Don't confuse depression with sadness. They are two very different emotions.

Sadness is the heaviness that comes from satiation. It is the state or condition of being "sated," of somehow being filled overfull. Sadness is the felt discomfort of that condition of satiation. Furthermore, it belongs to sadness to exaggerate itself, to play at itself, as Sartre observes: in one way or another, I always *make myself* sad.

In contrast, depression — true depression, not just sadness in one of its many self-posturing disguises — always comes unbidden, with nothing of pretense about it. In addition, it belongs to the experience of some important *loss*, some *giving up*, rather than to the experience of satisfaction. Depression is a hollowing out rather than an overfilling.

Depression occurs the other side of sadness. It might even be defined as the loss of all hope of ever reaching satiation or satisfaction — and, therefore, of the sadness that belongs to it.

Finally, sadness is always shortly followed by further search for satisfaction, as soon as the satiation wears off, whereas depression foreshadows acceptance and the rest that comes with it, as we will now consider.

---

attention to turn to other matters, such as being with loved ones, reconciling with family and friends where necessary, saying goodbye, and taking one's leave. Calm and serenity descend upon the dying person, even a certain joy, one chastened and purified of all frivolity. While still not at all happy to be dying, at this stage one is at least given the chance to die happy.

DEPRESSION, ACCEPTANCE, AND HAPPINESS

Borne with long enough — and even sometimes needing help through professional therapy or medication — depression eventually gives way and opens out into acceptance. As Elisabeth Kübler-Ross points out, acceptance is not as such a "happy stage," but is more nearly void of any feeling, positive or negative. Nevertheless, acceptance is an indispensable ingredient *in* happiness, at least of any solid and enduring sort: if we are unable to find acceptance when sorrow and suffering come our way, as they inevitably do, then any happiness we do attain will be precarious and doomed to eventual collapse.

Insofar as depression is a stage in the growth of acceptance itself, therefore, depression, borne patiently, can become the door leading to a lasting happiness.

Some alcoholics and addicts I have known in recovery who experience the "seven-year depression" (even if it doesn't come until the twentieth year — or comes early, during the first six) and are put on medication, as I was, to control it, are eventually able to come off the medication, as I was, without lapsing back into their premedicated state. Others have to continue taking medication. Still others do not need medication at all.

However, whether never, once, or still medicated for their depression, after they have borne with the condition for a time (sometimes a long time, sometimes not so long), something begins to happen to them about the eyes. At least that is what I think I have noticed. Their eyes become softer.

I've noticed, too, something about their voices. They become quieter, gentler, less raucous.

Finally, their general demeanor changes as well. Their gestures become less jerky and angular, more rounded and full. Soft, like their eyes, and gentle, like their voices. I hope it doesn't offend any of them for me to say so — I don't think it will — but I like them better since their depression. They give me more joy.

Self-Evaluation

To do a self-evaluation for this chapter, you can begin by asking yourself the following three basic questions:

1. How much sadness do you permit yourself? Asked in another way: to what degree do you manufacture your own sadness, or at least sustain and prolong it? What you are looking for is evidence of the degree to which you make *yourself* sad — the degree to which your sadness is a sort of role you play.

2. What have been your greatest sorrows, and what have they taught you? Pay particular attention to the second half of this question.

3. In your own experience with depression, did it gradually give way to acceptance? If not, what may have blocked it?

Disciplines, Practices, Exercises

Here are three exercises, one each for sadness, sorrow, and depression:

1. To lessen the sadness in your life, abandon your expectations. When you catch yourself forming expectations about how you yourself or others are supposed to act, just *drop* them.

2. Celebrate your sorrows. Give thanks for them; they show that you are still alive.

3. Accept your depressions. Wait patiently for acceptance.

– Nine –

Attention and the Enjoyment of the Emotions

We have to try to cure our faults by attention and not by will.
— Simone Weil, *Gravity and Grace*

Joy is the destiny of all emotion. Attention achieves that destiny.

To attend to an emotion is neither to encourage it nor to discourage it, neither to act it out nor to repress it, neither to praise nor to blame oneself for having it. To attend to an emotion is simply to let it be. In *Zen Mind, Beginner's Mind,* a popular classic of Buddhism in America, the Japanese Zen master Shunryu Suzuki says that the best way to control a cow or a sheep is to turn it loose in a large pasture. That is what it is to let something be: to turn it loose in a space ample enough for it to unfold itself freely. Attention is what turns emotion loose.

It is also what provides the pasture large enough for emotion fully to come into its own. Attention is what makes room for emotion, clears the way for it, opens up a space for it and keeps it open. Attention reserves and preserves a place for emotion, a place where emotion belongs, where it can be at home and free to be itself.

Then, let loose in the expanse attention spans — that is, opens, holds open, and keeps clear — for it, emotion is free to fulfill its destiny and become joy.

According to Jean-Paul Sartre, reflection poisons desire. No sooner do I catch sight of myself in the mirror of reflection than I begin to posture and pose. I try to *look* the part of one who desires. My focus has shifted from what I desire, the person or thing for which I long, to myself as the one desiring. I try to *be* that desiring one. I give up trying to attain what I began by desiring, instead concentrating on myself and on becoming "the one who desires." If I now actually attain what I desire, I find my success altogether *un*desirable, really no more than a bothersome distraction, diverting me from admiring myself in the mirror of my reflection.

A saying from the Christian desert fathers and mothers is that those who know they are praying are not really praying; only those who no longer know they are praying are really praying. The point is the same one Sartre is making.

As Sartre and the early Christian hermits knew, reflective awareness — *self-consciousness,* to speak everyday language — inserts itself between us and ourselves. Self-consciousness is an illness from which the self-conscious person suffers acutely. On that point, I can certainly speak with personal authority, since I have myself suffered acutely from self-consciousness all my life.

In front of a class teaching, talking over coffee with a friend, making small-talk at a party, riding next to a stranger on a plane — in fact, in any and every situation in which I find myself involved, self-consciousness constantly threatens to erupt on me unexpectedly, ruining everything. It comes suddenly, without warning, and typically at the worst possible moment. Absorbed in some activity, excited about it, wholly involved in what I'm doing, just when my passion and enthusiasm is about to peak, I am struck by self-consciousness, the reflective awareness *of* myself as "excited," "absorbed," "enthused," and at that very moment all direct involvement in what I am doing vanishes. I am hurled outside myself and transformed into no more than a spectator at my own life. When I am trapped in self-consciousness, I no longer really live my life at all; I just watch myself let it slip by.

Self-consciousness is a cloud always looking for a parade to rain on.

Such alienating, enervating, and deadening self-consciousness is anything but *attention,* which reconciles, enkindles, and enlivens. Self-consciousness, the reflective awareness of myself that is like looking at myself in a mirror, drives emotion away. It poisons emotion, whether that emotion be desire, as Sartre says, or the adoration at issue for a hermit in prayer. In contrast, attention does not drive emotion away, nor poison it. Rather, attention leaps ahead of emotion and clears the way for it. Attention welcomes emotion and makes it feel at ease, free to be itself fully and completely, for as long as it needs.

Attention detaches.

Self-consciousness *attaches* me to myself and my emotions. It makes me cling to myself like a whiny child to its mother, or like some especially wounded, needy person who attaches himself to me after I extend him some trivial kindness, dogging my footsteps and hanging all over me until I finally get fed up with him and drive him away in anger, only to punish myself with guilt for having done so. Like such an obnoxiously needy person, self-consciousness won't give me any room to breathe, to feel.

In contrast, attention *detaches* me from myself and my emotions. It gives me room to breathe and feel.

As our soul, which is air, holds us together, so wind and air encompass the whole world.   – ANAXIMENES, sixth century B.C.E.

Actually, at one level breathing and feeling are the same, since, as it were, emotion is the breath of daily human existence. The physical breath of the body unites inside and outside, ever exchanging each with the other, drawing the outside air in and bringing life-giving oxygen to the blood, then pushing the inside air out and carrying away the blood's toxic wastes. The breath is the body's moment-by-moment traffic with its environment, the body's incessant commerce with the earth and its elements, its intercourse with the physical world. That is why in one spiritual tradition after another the breath serves as a symbol for the spirit itself: what brings into community and commu-

ATTENTION AND SELF-CONSCIOUSNESS

Self-consciousness destroys attention. Attention and self-consciousness are opposites; they cannot coexist at one and the same place and time. Where the one is, the other cannot be. To be attentive to our own emotions is, therefore, anything but to be self-conscious about them. It is not even to be conscious that it is "I" who am having them. It is to attend to the *emotions themselves,* rather than to myself at all. It is, in effect, fully to *have* those emotions — fully to *feel* them. It is to have them, to feel them, *and no more.* That is, attention does not react to what is being felt; it just allows it to be felt, without distraction.

To be attentive to emotions, then, is "just" to feel them. However, though that may be simple, it is far from easy. We must constantly practice being "merely" attentive — that, and no "more."

nion; what enlivens and sustains; what reconciles and purifies; what enkindles and inflames; what links each to each and makes all one.

As the physical breath is the spirit of the body, emotion is the spirit of the soul. So long as it lives, the body is not without breath. At most, breathing can be arrested momentarily, "held" briefly, but never for long, and always followed by yet more vigorous breathing. In the same way, the human being is never without emotion. At most, one can arrest the play of emotion for a moment, becoming briefly emotionless by "numbing" oneself, perhaps — by "dissociating." But not for long, and emotion eventually reasserts itself with renewed vigor — the deeper and longer the numbness, the more violent and overpowering the resurgence when one finally does begin to feel again.

❖

My emotions show me how things are with me in the world moment by moment. They relate me to my world, and my world to me. They are no more "inside me" than my breath is; but they are also no more "outside me."

My anger *is* "how I am" toward the person toward whom I feel it — how I concretely *am* toward him or her at the moment I feel anger. It is not "inside" me; it *is* me — me as I am concretely at that moment *in relation to the other person at whom I am angry.* My anger binds me to the other person, and at the same time it reveals to me that I am so bound: that the other person has such claim on me, such power over me, that he or she can "make" me angry. My anger binds me to the other in such a way that the very bond between us — my anger itself — is what most of all presents itself to me.

When I am angry at some other person, I focus on that other person, to be sure. But my anger itself will not let me focus simply on that other person. Rather, my anger itself demands my attention. When I am angry I am no less focused on *myself,* as angry, than I am focused on the other person, who "makes" me angry. In fact, my anger forces me to focus on my own being in the world *with* that other person. It is only insofar as both I myself and the other person are concretely inseparable from our being together with one another in the world that, by forcing me to concentrate on how I am with and toward the other person at this very moment of anger, my anger forces me to concentrate simultaneously on myself and the other person.

My anger "demands my attention." As an emotion, it requires to be *felt.* That, after all, is what feelings are "for." Feelings are for feeling; they are to be felt. Truly to attend to a feeling is to feel it, nothing more and nothing less.

In a sense there is something remarkably *un*-natural about our "natural" responses to our feelings. Most of the time, the last thing we do, when we feel some emotion, is to attend to it simply as a feeling — that is, to let ourselves fully and completely feel it. Instead, most of the time we try to *drive our feelings away,* from the very moment we begin to feel them. We act as though becoming altogether *without* feeling were our ideal. But to be without feeling would be

EMOTIONS AND SELF-KNOWLEDGE

It is above all through my *emotions* that I am given knowledge of myself — of who I truly *am*. My emotions disclose me to myself as I am *concretely,* right now, in just *these* relationships with just *those* others who are there with me in just *this* situation at the moment. They give me knowledge of myself as I actually am at the moment I experience them. They tell me in great detail exactly "how things are" with me.

To understand what my emotions tell me about myself, however, I must know how to "read" them properly. I must be "emotionally literate."

to be dead, even if we were still walking around; it would be to be literally spiritless, without any breath of life.

So, to use examples already discussed in earlier chapters of this book, our apparently "natural" response to anger is to drive away what angers us; our "natural" response to fear is either to flee or to fight; our "natural" response to shame is to cover up; and our "natural" response to boredom is to seek distraction. In all these cases, our "natural" inclination is precisely to do what is designed to *eliminate* the given emotion as quickly and effectively as possible. When I manage to drive away the person who angers me, my anger ceases. When I manage to escape from what frightens me, my fear lets up. When I manage to cover my nakedness, I no longer blush in shame. When I succeed in distracting myself, I am no longer bored.

Since feelings, then, are by nature meant to be felt, by doing what seems to come so naturally to us as running away when we are frightened, we are in one sense acting contrary to nature. We are doing the very opposite to what feelings naturally demand of us. Instead of feeling our feelings, we are fleeing them — a most unnatural thing. In truth, our apparently "natural" response to emotion is no genuine *response* at all, but only a pure *reaction*. Any dog, cat, or rat can do the same — and always *does*, in fact. But human beings can also do something else, something that dogs, cats, and rats don't have as an option: they can *respond* to their own emotions, not merely react to them. Rather than simply being confined to "conditioned responses" (as psychologists sometimes call what I just called "reactions"), human beings can learn to make *free* responses. They can learn *not* to repeat their conditioning, but to answer creatively to the situation in which they find themselves.

To "respond" is to issue a *rejoinder*, in a very literal, twofold sense. First, we say that we "issue a rejoinder" when, for example, we reply to some charge that someone has made against us. In the same way, when we don't just react but respond to a situation, we are making a rejoinder in the sense of "replying" to the situation, "answering back" to it. Each new situation puts new questions to us, asking new things of us, and to respond to the situation is to answer back with replies to those questions.

At the same time, in answering the situation back, we also commit ourselves once again *to* and *in* the situation, we "join into" it again, again join ourselves to it, rejoin it. Thus, to put it all back together, genuinely to respond to a situation, rather than just to react to it as dictated by previous conditioning, is to rejoin ourselves to the situation in and through the rejoinder we make to the questions the situation puts to us.

Mindfulness, even of dissolution, is grounding. It is an experience of being strongly centered in the present and in oneself.
– ANNE C. KLEIN, "Presence with a Difference:
Buddhists and Feminists on Subjectivity,"
in Hypatia: A Journal of Feminist Philosophy (Fall 1994)

The rejoinder emotions call forth, the response for which they call, is to feel them, which we do, not when we self-consciously posture our emotions, but when we simply attend to them, letting them come

REACTING AND RESPONDING

A reaction is mechanical, automatic. It involves no choice or intention. It just happens automatically when triggered. There is no freedom involved, nor anything creative, regardless of whether the reaction is inborn or acquired. In a very basic sense, my reactions have nothing to do with "me," since they are merely mechanical formations.

A response, on the other hand, is free and creative. It issues a sort of "rejoinder" to what occasions it. My responses express me personally and always involve concrete choices and intentions.

and go as our concrete insertion in our situation determines moment by moment. To feel my emotions requires precisely that I dis-identify myself with them, dis-entangle myself from them. "Attention" is precisely the attitude in which I creatively disengage myself from my own emotions, thereby giving them breathing space to be felt, and myself breathing space to feel them.

Attention — "mindfulness" in the Buddhist tradition, *nepsis* or "watchfulness" in the Orthodox Christian monastic tradition — is pure nonjudgmental awareness. It is nonjudgmental awareness in two directions simultaneously. On the one hand, attention is awareness of the situation in which experience occurs. It is awareness of the *contents* of experience. On the other hand, attention is at the same time awareness of the *quality of experience itself,* the quality of the experience *of* those very contents. Attention is wide-awake awareness of the moment-by-moment interplay of "world" and "self," of the concrete *incarnation* of the self *in* the world.

To pay attention to one's emotions (to be "mindful" of them, "watchful" toward them) is neither to lose oneself in them, acting them out, nor to deny that one has them, repressing them beneath the level of articulate awareness. It is, instead, to treat them as an attentive parent treats a small child. Such a parent is always acutely aware of the child, at all times knowing precisely where the child is and what the child is doing. At the same time, the attentive parent is sharply aware of the smallest details of the surroundings, alert to any signs of danger for the child. Yet the parent's awareness of child and environment has nothing of anxiousness about it; it is very relaxed. Furthermore, without sacrificing the least awareness of the child and the surroundings, the parent may well be actively involved in some activity of the parent's own, such as talking with a friend. Finally, and most importantly, the attentive parent is careful not to interfere with the child and the child's immersion in its own activities. Indeed, the whole purpose of the parent's attentiveness is to assure the child a safe and supporting space to be left alone by herself or himself, to explore and experiment freely.

To pay attention to our emotions is to treat them in the same way. It is to provide them room to unfold themselves and be felt, provide them room to be felt by providing ourselves room to feel them.

Watchfulness is a continual fixing and halting of thought at the entrance to the heart.

    – HESYCHIOS OF SINAI, Orthodox Saint, *On Watchfulness and Holiness*

Emotions blossom under the light of attention. They open up and spread themselves out when we attend to them. In the process our emotions transform themselves. Like a shy person coming out of the shell when made to feel accepted and welcome, and becoming the life of the party, even the most taciturn emotions become loquacious. In time, they even start to sing.

Given enough attention anger cools down. Attention reveals anger as frustrated compassion, and compassion is just what anger eventually becomes, given enough attention. Very slowly, but as sure as it is slow, attention transforms anger into compassion.

As for fear, attention transforms fear into love. Attention transforms boredom into fidelity, shame into modesty, and sadness into the joy of sorrow. Attention lets all such "distressing" emotions, as Aristotle calls them, relax, letting all the distress go. In my letting go of my being distressed by it, distressed emotion is freed to let itself go; and when distressed emotion lets itself go, what suddenly, unexpectedly comes to fill the space is joy. Attention en-joys the emotions: it turns them all into joy.

Joy is not one emotion alongside all the others. Rather, joy is the very heart of emotion. It beats in all emotions, even the most distressed, distressing ones.

Compassion, which anger becomes when attended to long enough, is joyful. So is fidelity, to which boredom gives way when warmed sufficiently by attention. Sorrow, as I discussed in the last chapter, is its own form of joy, the form into which attention lets sadness open. And the authentic modesty into which attention transforms shame is always joyful, just as authentic joy is always modest: joy doesn't seek to make any fuss about itself, but only about what it takes joy in.

Joy also spreads. Joy is a fire that leaps up and dances, bursting into flame and inflaming in turn whatever comes into contact with it. But like the burning bush of Moses — or like love, which is just one of the forms it takes — joy burns without consuming. It never burns up what it sets afire.

The only reason to become literate is so that one can read. The only reason to become emotionally literate is so that one can feel. Attention is the way to feel, as scanning with the eyes or, in braille, the fingertips is the way to read.

The more one reads, the more one enjoys reading; the more one feels, the more one enjoys feeling. Above all, the more one travels the road of attention, which lets one feel, the more one is en-joyed.

The story goes that Father Lot came to Father Joseph and said, "Father, as my strength permits I keep a little rule of devotion. I pray and fast and meditate in quiet. As I am able, I keep watch over my thoughts and my imaginings, purging them as necessary. What more must I do?" The old man, Father Joseph, rose. He held his hands up

ATTENTION AND JOY

Joy is not just another emotion along with fear and anger and all the rest. Joy is, as it were, the emotion toward which all the others are pointing, as toward their own fulfillment and completion. Joy is the destiny of *all* emotion.

Attention — the "mindfulness" of Buddhism, the "watchfulness" of Orthodox Christianity — is what gives emotions that proper care and room to develop. It is, in effect, what empowers emotion to fulfill its destiny and become joy. Attention transforms emotion into joy.

against the sky and spread them wide. His fingers became like ten tongues of flame against the sun. "If you will," he told the younger man in an awed whisper, "you can become pure fire."

So can we all.

Self-Evaluation

The question to direct you in the final self-evaluation of this book will not take me long at all to ask, but it will take you all the rest of your life to answer, if you care to. Here's the question:

How much joy can you stand in your life?

Disciplines, Practices, Exercises

Practice the following exercise until you answer the question just asked.

- Be attentive ("mindful," "watchful") to whatever emotions you may come to feel, whenever you feel them. Keep doing this until you are given no more to feel.